Coaching the Single Wing Offense

Jim Ahern

ISBN: 1-58518-912-X
Library of Congress Control Number: 2004112389
Cover design: Jeanne Hamilton
Book layout: Jeanne Hamilton

Coaches Choice
P.O. Box 1828
Monterey, CA 93942
www.coacheschoice.com

Dedication

Three groups of people have made it possible for me to survive in the competitive world of football coaching. The first are the players that have played for me during over thirty years of coaching football. I have been fortunate to have hard working, committed athletes that knew the effort that was required to be successful both on and off the field. I have always said, "You can't make a cherry pie, without some cherries."

My assistant coaches are the second group that I owe a great deal of gratitude. Some of them have put up with me for over 28 years. Mike Doran and L.D. Jones have been recognized as Assistant Coach of the Year by the MHSFCA. Others, like Terry Hessbrook, Craig Snyder, and Rich Ebright, have played for me and have returned to coach at their alma mater. My assistants' dedication and loyalty to the program are a big reason for its success. Most successful programs have stability in their coaching staffs, and I've been fortunate to have that luxury here at Ithaca Public Schools.

The final group is the most important to me. It is my family. My wife Gerri has been at every game and has endured the rigors of being a coach's wife for over 36 years. She is my strength, my biggest fan (and sometimes critic when I need it), and the love of my life. My son Mike played for me and, even though a successful physicians assistant, finds time to help me coach. He has made me look good for quite a few years. My oldest daughter Kristyn was my biggest cheerleader. Death from a rare heart disease took her from us at the young age of 19; but I'm sure as she looks down at us she is leading the angels in cheers for the Yellowjackets. My youngest daughter Julie not only cheered for dad's team, but kept stats, too. She kept dad in line and always had the right thing to say after a tough loss or a great victory. Even though she is a busy social worker today, she still finds time to be at almost every game to continue supporting the "old coach."

These three groups are very important to me, and I would not be where I am today without them. Thank you to all of them.

Contents

Dedication 3

Introduction 6

Chapter 1   Basic Organization 9

Chapter 2   Line Play 22

Chapter 3   Backfield Play 34

Chapter 4   The Spin Series 40

Chapter 5   The Power Series 48

Chapter 6   The Motion Series 56

Chapter 7   The Buck Lateral Series 63

Chapter 8   Supplemental Plays 71

Chapter 9   The Passing Game 76

Chapter 10   The Spread Single Wing 92

Chapter 11   The Secret Weapon 109

Conclusion 111

About the Author 112

Introduction

"What do you run on offense?" Whenever coaches get together, that question is sure to come up in the conversation. When I tell them that I run the single wing, many will give a look of disbelief and say, "Right! What do you really run?" After a short time talking with them, putting the offense down on paper, and asking them how they would defense it, the looks of disbelief become looks of excitement, and they want to know more about the offense. I'm writing this book for that reason. When we first went to the single wing, I tried to find as much information about the offense as I could. To say the least, it was quite difficult. About the only information available were some articles that I found in old coaching magazines. These articles were helpful, but didn't give me the in-depth information I was looking for. Most of the books that had been written on the single wing were no longer in print, and I couldn't find them in the libraries. Due to the fact that I couldn't find written material on the single wing, I turned to coaches that were running or had run the offense. Many coaches exist that are much more qualified than I am to write about the single wing. Most of the information in this book I learned from them. Some of these coaches helped me a great deal when I first began to run the offense. I will always be indebted to John Aldrich, Keith Piper, Ken Keuffel, Bob Howard, Ken Hofer, Dan Johnson, Carl Fetters, George Rykovich, Pat Egan, Norris Patterson, Jerry Carle, Ted Hern, Marvin Wetzel, Mark Bliss, Steve Ragsdale, and many others that have been very, very successful in running the single wing offense and were willing to share their knowledge with me. In fact, much of the way we run the single wing is a compilation of things I have learned from other coaches. Very little of what we do is original thinking. However, we have been successful with what we are doing, and hopefully this book will give a coach that is thinking about running the single wing a starting point to put this offense into his program.

Before going into the advantages of the single wing offense, let me explain how we got into the offense in the first place. I began coaching in 1967 and most of my early coaching experience was in running the option offense in some form. We ran from an unbalanced line most of the time. If the defense adjusted to the strongside, we wanted to run the veer option to the shortside. Or, if the defense didn't adjust, we had them outnumbered to the strongside when running the sweep and power game.

In the 1993 season, we had a small quarterback that was good at running the option, but had trouble seeing in definite passing situations. To help him, we installed the shotgun formation so that he could see the field better. So that defenses wouldn't know that we were going to pass every time we got into the shotgun formation, we installed three single wing run plays to keep the defense honest. In the fifth game, our quarterback runs a bootleg, but slips and injures his knee. We didn't really have a true backup option quarterback, thus, behind at halftime 0-21, we decided to go to the shotgun for the second half. Instead of the backup quarterback, we decided to play the third-string tight end, who was also a good passer. His only live experience throwing was against the secondary in skelly practice, but he knew the single wing plays. To make a long story short, we almost won the game against a team that had only given up three touchdowns up to that point in the season. We scored three second-half touchdowns. The final score was 28-21.

At our coaching meeting that weekend, we decided to stay with what we were doing, expand on it, and see what would happen. The team won its last four games (three of which wouldn't have been won with the old offense). In the off-season, the decision was made to go with the single wing. Thus began the quest for information about the offense and, in a roundabout way, the reason for this book.

Many advantages exist when running the single wing. Some of them are unfamiliarity, simplicity, adaptability, deception, power, passing, quick kicking, and unusual formations. Following is a summary of these advantages.

One of the biggest advantages is unfamiliarity. Opponents most likely won't see the offense more than once a year. Preparing for it and trying to simulate it in practice is very difficult because the offense is so different from what they normally see. A week isn't much time to get ready for it without neglecting other parts of their game.

Simplicity is another big advantage of the single wing offense. At any level of football, the team that makes the fewest mistakes is usually the winner. One of the biggest advantages of the single wing offense is that it doesn't ask an average player to do something he can't do. The blocking schemes are very simple, and, for most plays, a double-team at the point of attack is involved. The offense also doesn't put so much pressure on one back to carry the load, as all of the backs are involved in the single wing.

At every level of football, especially the high school or lower levels, the coach should select an offense that is suitable to his current personnel. This adaptability is a major strength of the single wing offense. To make the offense work doesn't require highly skilled players. The line doesn't have to be big and powerful, and the backs don't have to have exceptional speed to make the offense work. Obviously, the better the players the better the offense will work. The single wing offense is also very adaptable and allows the coach to highlight different positions from year to year, depending on personnel, without changing the offense.

Deception is another advantage of the single wing. The deception of the spinner series holds linebackers and secondary for an extra second and allows the blockers to get position and execute their block. Many times, a linebacker or secondary person will go the wrong way because they couldn't find the ball.

The single wing allows a team to amass a lot of power at the point of attack. As an example, the single wing allows the offense to add one more blocker than normal at the point of attack.

The single wing allows for excellent passing. Many of the modern college and pro teams utilize shotgun formations when they have to pass. The shotgun is a version of the single wing. Without altering the formation, the single wing allows a team to get four receivers into the pattern quickly. Also, the defense still has to guess as to whether the play is going to be a pass or a run.

The single wing is also an excellent formation from which to quick kick. Although not used by many teams, the change in field position that can be gained from its use has been the difference in many ball games.

Another big advantage of the single wing is that many different formations can be used to add to the defense's problems. Motion can also be used as a weapon to confuse the defense. Although different formations and motion makes the defense adjust, almost all plays can be run from the different formations to take advantage of the adjustments that the defense is or isn't making. Even something as simple as going from an unbalanced right formation to an unbalanced left formation can cause even a well-coached team adjustment problems at times. The headaches that the different single wing formations can cause an opponent's defense is amazing.

1

Basic Organization

Selection of Personnel

As with any offense, certain types of players are best suited for certain positions on the team. Following is a brief description of the qualities that are necessary for each of the offensive positions in the single wing offense, as shown in Diagram 1-1.

QE QG C PG QT PT PE
        (BLOCKING BACK)   (WING BACK)
             1 BACK   3 BACK
(TAILBACK) (QUARTERBACK)
   4 BACK 2 BACK

Diagram 1-1

Quick End

The quick end should be the best receiving end. Although he should also be a good blocker, blocking is not as important as having quickness and the ability to catch the ball. Most of his blocks are leading through the hole, down-field, linebackers, or double-teams.

Quick Guard

The quick guard is usually the smallest interior lineman. Most of his blocks are against linebackers or double-teams. Many times the quick guards are former backs that don't quite have enough speed to be a back, but are too good of a player not to have on the field somewhere.

Center

The main job of the center is to get a perfect snap every time. The blocks that he has are either double-teams or away from the point of attack. He will never have to block a man that is head up on him alone. Size is not a factor as much as quick feet. His toughest blocks are on pass plays, but, in most cases, he will have someone helping him. The center is a good spot for the player that has a lot of heart, but is not blessed with a lot of talent. His main responsibility is the snap. Everything else is secondary.

Power Guard

The power guard must be able to trap block, as he will be pulling on many of the 1 and 2 hole plays. He must also have the ability to recognize defensive alignment quickly, as he will be the one that starts the line calls on the 1 and 2 holes. Size is not as important as quickness, as most of his blocks are double-teams, down blocks, or traps. Although similar to the quick guard in quickness, the power guard is usually stronger and bigger.

Quick Tackle

The quick tackle is usually one of the bigger and best linemen. The quick tackle must be able to execute the short trap, because his block is key on all 5 and 6 hole plays. He must also be able to pull for some 1 and 2 hole plays depending on the defensive alignment, but due to his alignment, these blocks are short traps.

Power Tackle

As the name indicates, this position is for the biggest and strongest lineman. The power tackle is usually the best one-on-one blocker. This position is the only player that is asked to sometimes block a defensive player alone that is head up on him. The better this player is, the better the offense will be able to run the 1 and 2 holes. Against some defensive alignments, he may have to pull on the 1 and 2 holes; but, it is a very short pull, being not much more than a cross block with the power end. Like the quick tackle, the power tackle is usually one of the best linemen, just not as quick.

Power End

The power end would be the typical tight end in most offenses. The power end is required to block down on linemen or linebackers, with the block being a double-team in many cases. He is also asked to catch the ball, usually on short routes. The power end is usually bigger than the quick end, and he should be a better blocker. He should have the ability to pull and lead through a hole, which is his responsibility on the 7 hole.

Blocking Back

The blocking back position is a combination of the power guard and power end positions. Since most of his blocks are against linebackers, size isn't as important as toughness. Many times the blocking back is also the middle linebacker on defense. He should be a good blocker, as he will be leading the way on many plays. The blocking back should also be able to catch the ball, as he is a primary receiver on many of the pass plays. This position is very important in the single wing offense.

Wingback

The first quality required for the wingback is speed. The wingback is primarily a runner and pass receiver. He does block on some plays, but size isn't a factor on his blocks. This position can be a game breaker. The wingback usually has the best average per carry and per reception on the team. The better the wingback, the better the offensive production will be. The wingback should also be willing to fake, which is an important part of the offense.

Tailback

The tailback is the best runner. He will carry the ball outside and inside. Obviously, size and speed are desired at this position. The tailback's key ability should be reading his blocks and cutting off of them. The more illusive he is in the open field the better, because he will find himself in that situation a lot in this offense. The tailback is also required to catch the ball some, usually on screens or flare passes. The tailback will be asked to block some, usually on pass plays. As with all of the backs, he should fake extremely well to make the offense succeed. At the end of the season, the leading ground gainer should be the tailback.

Quarterback

The quarterback (sometimes called spinback or fullback by other single wing coaches) is the most skilled position on the team. His leadership on the field is extremely important. He must be a runner, passer, and a very good faker. Most quarterbacks would be halfbacks or tailbacks in other offenses. The quarterback has many of the same qualities as option quarterbacks. He will handle the ball on most of the plays in the offense. Although he will run the ball more than throw it, he should be able to throw the ball to keep the defense honest. While the quarterback need not be a great passer, he must be able to throw the short play-action passes to keep the defense guessing. The quarterback can be any type and size. Some are better runners, while others are better passers. At the end of the season however, the total offensive leader is usually the quarterback.

Huddle Organization

The quarterback is in charge of the huddle. Once he steps into the huddle, no other players should talk. The quarterback will have his back to the line of scrimmage, while the rest of the team will be facing the line of scrimmage. The quarterback will be five yards from the line of scrimmage, as shown in Diagram 1-2.

LINE OF SCRIMMAGE

THE HUDDLE IS 5 YDS. FROM THE L.O.S.

2

PT QT PG C QG
PE 3 1 4 QE

Diagram 1-2. The huddle

Play Calling

The quarterback will call the play in the following manner: first, he will give the formation; second, he will give the play by saying three numbers. The first number is who will receive the snap; the second number is who will carry the ball; and the third number is the hole. An example of this type of play call is, "Blue, 241." After the quarterback has given the information, the center will leave the huddle and get set at the line of scrimmage. The quarterback will repeat the information and give the command, "Ready." The rest of the team will clap their hands and answer, "Score," then hurry to the line of scrimmage and get set.

Cadence

The cadence is non-rhythmic. The quarterback calls out the number of safeties (one, two, or zero), then yells, "Set, go." The ball is snapped on "go" most of the time. When the defense is starting to anticipate the snap, the quarterback can call long count in the huddle. While this call is not used a lot, when long count is used, the defense almost always receives a penalty. If long count is called in the huddle, the quarterback always says, "Listen to the count," before giving the play (for example: "Listen to the count. Blue, 241, long count"). At the line of scrimmage, the quarterback will try to draw the defense offside by really accentuating the "go." If the defense doesn't jump, the quarterback will try again to pull them offside a couple of times, then give a color, which indicates the snap is on the next "go." The call would happen like this: "Set, go, go, go, go, go!, red, go." This method can be very effective to keep the defense from anticipating the snap count.

Hole Numbering

The holes are numbered from the power end toward the quick end. In a red formation (R for right), the 1 hole would be to the right, or toward the power end. In a blue formation, the 1 hole would be to the left, again toward the power end. These methods of hole numbering are shown in Diagrams 1-3 and 1-4.

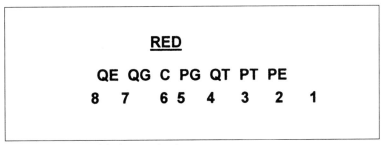

Diagram 1-3. Blue hole numbering

Diagram 1-4. Red hole numbering

Formations

In all formations, the formation is preceded by a color, red or blue. The color tells the line where they should line up. The base formation is blue or red. If the quarterback just says "blue" or "red," the formation is the normal single wing alignment. The coach can dream up many formations with the single wing. The coach should make sure that he has a purpose with each one he creates. A lot of different formations can be used during a game to see how the defense is going to adjust. As mentioned previously, an advantage of the single wing is that most of the offense can be run from each of the different formations. This system puts a lot of pressure on the defense, because preparing for the base single wing offense is tough, let alone all the other different formations that are possible. Diagrams 1-5 and 1-6 illustrate the main formations in the single wing offense.

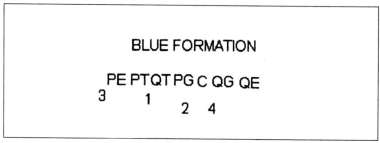

Diagram 1-5. Blue formation

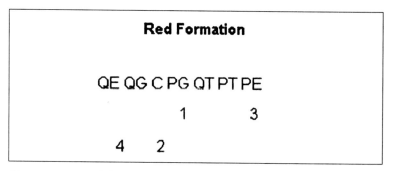

Diagram 1-6. Red formation

The basic line splits are six inches from the power end to the quick end. Variances in the line splits are possible, depending on the play. However, the tight splits help the blocking schemes, both for the run and pass, and make blitzing tougher. The line will immediately get into their three-point stance upon reaching the line of scrimmage, with their down hand even with the center's heels.

The wingback is one yard outside the power end and one yard deep. The blocking back's base alignment is between the quick tackle and power tackle, one yard deep. However, he may move around depending on the play. The quarterback's alignment straddles the inside leg of the power guard, at a depth of 3.5 yards from the ball. The tailback's alignment is anywhere from straddling the inside leg of the quick guard to being in the quick guard-quick end gap, based on his speed. He will have his heels on the toes of the quarterback. The quarterback and tailback are aligned closer to the line than many teams that run the single wing. They align that way because more deception on fakes is possible, and they can hit the hole quicker, which makes blocking for the line easier. The quarterback and the tailback are both looking at the ball. All of the backs are in a two-point stance. This formation creates more deception, and makes the center's snaps easier.

New formations can be made by the back or backs immediately going to their new set upon breaking the huddle. Backs can also be put in motion to create a new formation. In some cases, the motion is determined by the play called, for example, "224 motion." At other times, a back can be put in motion by the quarterback calling his number and the type of motion required. The word "motion" alone tells the back to motion across the formation from his original alignment. The term S-motion tells the back to motion to the sideline on the same side as his original alignment. The term Z-motion tells the back to go across the formation halfway and return to his original alignment. These types of motion are shown in Diagrams 1-7 through 1-9.

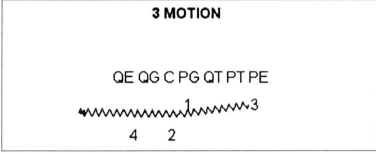
Diagram 1-7. 3 motion

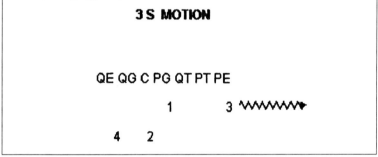
Diagram 1-8. 3 S-motion

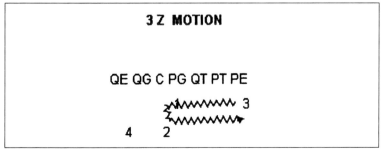
Diagram 1-9. 3 Z-motion

Blue Flanker (Power or Quick)

The term flanker puts the 3 back to a position 10 yards outside either the quick or power end, as shown in Diagram 1-10.

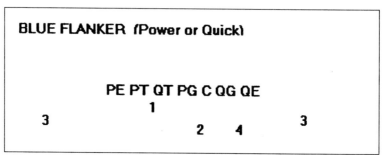

Diagram 1-10. Flanker power or flanker quick

Over

The term over tells the 1 back to align on the inside leg of the quick end, as shown in Diagram 1-11. This formation is a power set that puts a lot of pressure on the defense. If they don't adjust, they can be hurt quickly to the quick side. This formation still allows the offense to run all plays to the power side.

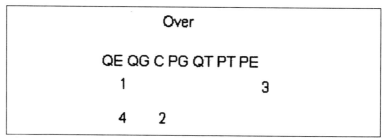

Diagram 1-11. Over

Wing

The term wing tells the 3 back to align one yard outside the quick end and one yard deep, as shown in Diagram 1-12. Like the over formation, wing puts immediate pressure on the defense to the quick side, but still allows all plays to be run to the power side.

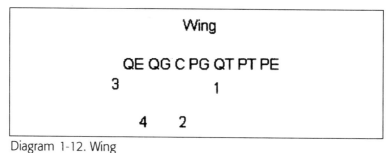

Diagram 1-12. Wing

Wing-Over

The term wing-over brings both the 1 back and 3 back to the quick side, where they align as they would in the over and in the wing, as shown in Diagram 1-13. If the defense doesn't adjust, they are in big trouble to the quick side, but the offense can still run all plays to the power side.

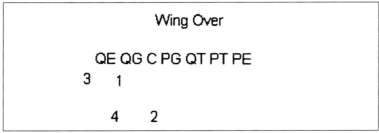

Diagram 1-13. Wing-over

Pro

The term pro tells the quick end and the 3 back to split 10 yards wider than their original alignments, as shown in Diagram 1-14. This alignment is a strong running formation to the power side and a good set to run the option to the quick side. Pro is also a passing formation.

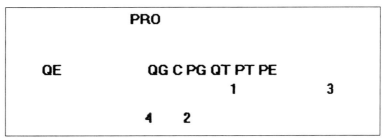

Diagram 1-14. Pro

1 Pro

The term 1 pro tells the 1 back to take the 3 back's pro alignment and tells the 3 back to stay in his original alignment, as shown in Diagram 1-15. This alignment is a strong passing formation with a trips set to the power side. Also, 1 pro is a strong running formation, especially for the 1 hole, with the potential of a crack back block by the 1 back to seal the inside. The option to the quick side is a threat, especially if the secondary makes a strong commitment to the trips side.

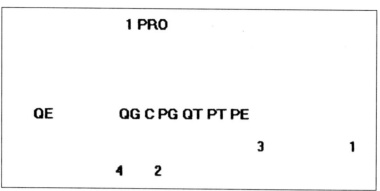

Diagram 1-15. 1 pro

Twins

The term twins tells the quick end to align in the pro set and the 3 back to align two to five yards inside of the quick end, as shown in Diagram 1-16. Twins is a strong passing set to the quick side. This set is also a good formation to run the option, with the 3 back being the extra blocker. If the defense adjusts to the quick side, they are vulnerable to the power side running game.

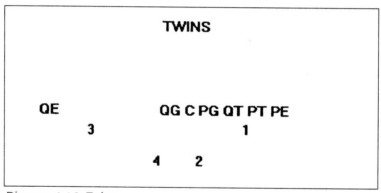

Diagram 1-16. Twins

Twins-Over

The term twins-over tells the 1 back to align in the over set and the quick end and 3 back to align in the twins set, as shown in Diagram 1-17. This alignment is a spread version of the wing-over formation, with the same advantages. Twins-over forces the defense to adjust either to the power or quick side.

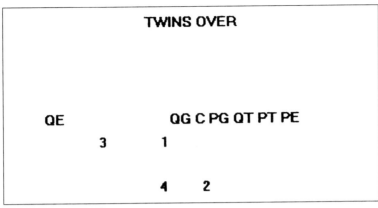

TWINS OVER

QE   QG C PG QT PT PE

3   1

4   2

Diagram 1-17. Twins-over

Trips

The term trips tells the quick end to align in the pro alignment, the 3 back to align five yards inside of the quick end, and the 1 back three yards inside of the 3 back, as shown in Diagram 1-18. This alignment is a very strong formation to the quick side for either the pass or run. However, much of the offense can still be run to the power side.

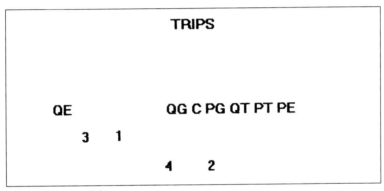

TRIPS

QE   QG C PG QT PT PE

3   1

4   2

Diagram 1-18. Trips

1 Trips

The term 1 trips tells the 1 back and the 4 back to switch from their alignment in trips, as shown in Diagram 1-19. Although the formation looks just like trips to the defense and can be used much the same way, the main objective is to get a stronger blocker (the 1 back) and a faster receiver (the 4 back) into positions where they can best help the offense. The drawback is that this formation doesn't allow for many plays to be run back to the power side without the use of motion.

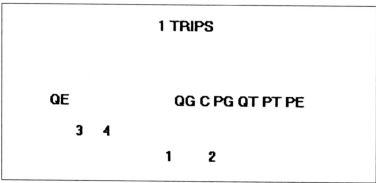

Diagram 1-19. 1 trips

Trey

Trey is a very powerful formation from which to run the power series, especially the 1 hole, as shown in Diagram 1-20. This set is a strong passing formation to the power side. Also, because of possible defensive adjustments to the power side, counters and options to the quick side are very effective.

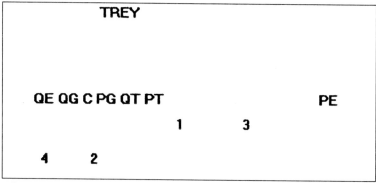

Diagram 1-20. Trey

Deuce

This alignment is the favorite formation for running the hurry-up offense with no huddle, as shown in Diagram 1-21. While mainly used for the passing game, deuce allows the quarterback to still run inside plays. And, with motion (or a 1 deuce where the 1 back and 4 back switch alignments), other running plays can be run by the other backs.

These formations are only the main alignments, with a variety of other possible formations existing. The coach should use at least three or four formations in each game to force the defense to make adjustments. And, this variety of sets forces future opponents to guess about the formations for which they'll need to prepare.

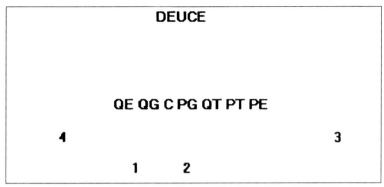

Diagram 1-21. Deuce

Automatic System

Two different types of automatic systems are utilized. The first is a "check with me" system. In this system, the play is actually called at the line of scrimmage. This system is used against teams that may use a special defense in certain situations that may leave it vulnerable to a particular play. Or, it may be used to run away from a particular player that the defense moves around from play to play. Going into the game, the quarterback will be taught two plays from which to choose. In the first example, the choices might be between a run or a play-action pass off of that run action in a short yardage situation. In the second example, the choices might be one play to one side or another play to the opposite side, depending on where the defensive player is aligned. In the huddle, the quarterback says, "Check with me." Then at the line of scrimmage, the quarterback will give a color (which means nothing in this case) and call the play. The snap count is always on "go."

The other automatic system is used in the hurry-up or two-minute offense. The offense will not huddle in the hurry-up offense. In this system, a live color and a base play are determined. If the live color isn't called at the line of scrimmage, the base play is run. For example, if the live color is red and the quarterback calls any other color, the play is ignored and the base play is run. If, on the other hand, the quarterback calls "red," which is the live color, the play called is run. Again, the ball is always snapped on "go."

These systems are very useful, and both are easy for the players. A coach doesn't want to find himself in situations where his team isn't in control at critical game times. Both of these automatic systems give the offense an edge in games and become a big factor in the final outcome.

Line Play

The success of any offense always begins with the offensive line. As mentioned in the Introduction, the line play is simple and fun for the linemen. No player is asked to perform a block that he isn't capable of executing. This book is not a technique manual on line play. Many texts are available on the subject of line play. Rather, this chapter will concentrate on the blocking schemes that are used for each of the single wing run holes.

The Center

"Isn't there a problem with the center snap?" is a question often asked of single wing coaches. From experience, it can honestly be said that fewer bad snaps occur with the single wing snap from the center than with the traditional quarterback-center exchange. Also, when a bad snap has occurred, the offense doesn't lose the ball because it's away from the line of scrimmage. Keeping the ball usually isn't the case with the traditional quarterback-center exchange. The actual snap for the center is easy, because the snap is only 3.5 yards. For more traditional single wing sets, the snap will be about 4.5 yards. The most important part of the snap is accuracy. A common single wing series is the spin series, which is most effective when the fake holds the defense for an extra split second as they try to find the ball. The snap plays a key part in the deception. The snap should be low, between the quarterback's knee and thigh. This position allows the quarterback to stay low and perform his spin technique with as much deception as possible. The center doesn't have to be a great lineman, but does have to perform the snap consistently.

When single wing coaches get together, a discussion usually occurs as to whether the center should look back at the quarterback or keep his head-up, looking at the defense. This book recommends that the center snap the ball while looking at the defense. With the center's head-up, the snaps are still accurate, and the center is a more effective blocker, especially on pass blocking.

Another discussion among single wing coaches is whether to have the center snap with two hands or one hand. The best approach is to let the center decide which method he prefers, as long as he is accurate with the snap. Most centers will use the one-hand method because it feels more natural.

As was previously stated, in the selection of personnel, the center is chosen not because he is a great lineman, but because of his heart. This position is for the lineman that probably wouldn't play in another style of offense, but is willing to work at perfecting the snap so it is accurate every time.

Terminology

Following is an explanation of the terminology used in describing the different line blocks in the single wing.

Head to Playside

In most single wing blocks, for both the run and pass, the blocker must strive to have his head between the defender and the point of attack. The blocker should have his head on the same side of the defender as the direction of the play or to the side where the quarterback is throwing the ball. The exception occurs on a run, when the lineman is going to block the defender alone, and the defender that is going to be blocked is to the lineman's inside, and the ball is going outside of him. In this case, the blocker must stop the defender's penetration, thus the lineman's head should be in front of the defender as he drives the defender down the line. As an aiming point, the lineman should step with his inside foot at the defender's far foot.

Man—Lineman—Linebacker

The term "man" means either a lineman or a linebacker (for example, "Block the first man to the inside"). If a choice has to be made between a lineman and a linebacker, in a stack for example, always choose the lineman. Cross the player's face rule: if due to defensive movement (for example, a cross stunt from a stack), he should block the first defender that crosses in front of him.

The term "lineman" means a defender with his hand on the ground. For example, in the statement, "Block the first lineman to the inside," the lineman might be a defensive tackle.

The term "linebacker" means a man in a two-point stance and off the line of scrimmage. For example, in the statement, "Block the first linebacker to the inside," the player to block might be a middle linebacker.

Red Zone

The power guard, quick tackle, and power tackle each have a red zone or area of responsibility for the 1 and 2 holes. Each of the linemen knows that if his red zone has a lineman in it, he cannot pull to block at the point of attack. Blocking the red zone always takes priority over pulling. The power guard, quick tackle, and power tackle will make a call on every play, but they are only live on the 1 and 2 holes. Each lineman's red zone is from their inside shoulder to head-up on the man to their inside.

Power Guard's Calls

The red zone for the power guard is from head-up on the center to his inside shoulder. If no lineman is in the red zone, the power guard gives a "me" call and pulls to block at the point of attack. If a lineman is in the red zone, the power guard gives a "you" call and blocks the lineman in the red zone. The power guard's calls are shown in Diagrams 2-1 and 2-2.

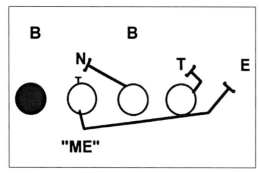

Diagram 2-1. "Me" call

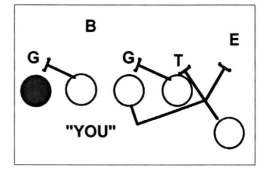

Diagram 2-2. "You" call

Quick Tackle's Calls

The red zone for the quick tackle is from head-up on the power guard to his inside shoulder. If the power guard gives a "me" call, the quick tackle will answer with a "gap" call and block the first lineman from his red zone to the outside. If the power guard gives a "you" call, the quick tackle must check his red zone to make his call. If no lineman is in the red zone, the quick tackle gives a "me" call, pulls, and blocks at the point of attack. If a lineman is in his red zone, the quick tackle gives a "you" call and blocks the lineman in the red zone. The quick tackle's calls are shown in Diagrams 2-3, 2-4, and 2-5.

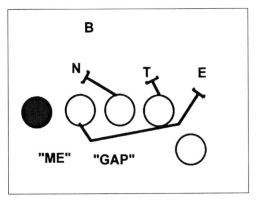

Diagram 2-3. "Me" and "gap" calls

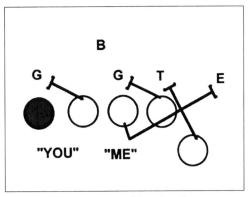

Diagram 2-4. "You" and "me" calls

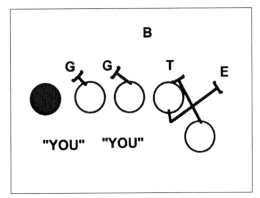

Diagram 2-5. "You" and "you" calls

Power Tackle's Calls

The red zone for the power tackle is from head-up on the quick tackle to his inside shoulder. If the quick tackle gives a "gap" or "me" call, the power tackle will answer with a "gap" call and block the first lineman from his red zone to the outside. If the quick tackle gives a "you" call, the power tackle must check his red zone to make his call. If no lineman is in the red zone, the power tackle gives a "me" call, pulls, and blocks at the point of attack. If a lineman is in the red zone, the power tackle gives a "rock" call and blocks the lineman in the red zone. The "rock" call alerts the 1 back to block at the point of attack instead of the linebacker and the quick end to look inside for a linebacker before blocking the corner or safety. The power tackle's calls are shown in Diagrams 2-6 through 2-9.

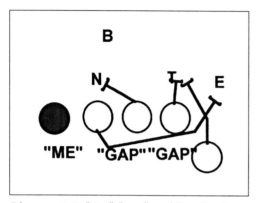
Diagram 2-6. "Me," "gap," and "gap" calls

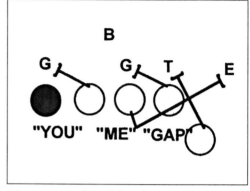
Diagram 2-7. "You," "me," and "gap" calls

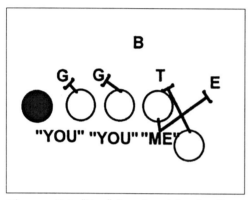
Diagram 2-8. "You," "you," and "me" calls

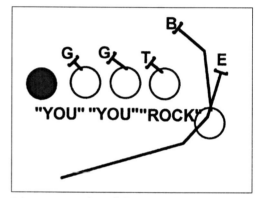
Diagram 2-9. "You," "you," and "rock" calls

Summary of Line Calls and Answers

Power guard:	"me" or "you"
Quick tackle:	Answers "me" with "gap"
	Answers "you" with "me" or "you"
Power tackle:	Answers "me" or "gap" with "gap"
	Answers "you" with "me" or "rock"
1 back:	"Rock" call tells him to block at the point of attack instead of the linebacker
Quick end:	"Rock" call tells him to check inside for a linebacker before blocking a Corner or Safety

"Gap" Call

The "gap" call is used by the quick tackle and power tackle on the 1 and 2 holes as explained previously. Also, the quick guard uses this call on the 8 hole. The quick guard on the 8 hole will make the call if he has a lineman from head-up on the center to his inside gap and has a lineman in his outside gap. This call tells the 1 back on the 8 hole to block the first lineman from head-up on the man making the call to the outside, instead of blocking the linebacker. The "gap" call is shown in Diagram 2-10.

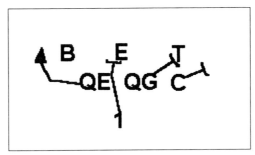

Diagram 2-10. "Gap" call

Combo Block

This block is usually used on pass plays, but can also be used on running plays. The combo block is used when one lineman has a linebacker and the lineman next to him has a lineman to block on the play. Both linemen will drive into the lineman as they keep an eye on the linebacker. If the linebacker blitzes, one of the players will slide off the lineman and pick up the linebacker, while the other stays with the lineman. If the linebacker doesn't blitz, both players will stay with the lineman. Usually used by the power or quick guard and center on pass blocking, this block is occasionally used by all linemen. Diagram 2-11 illustrates the combo block.

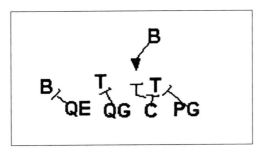

Diagram 2-11. Combo block

Fold Block

Although this block is seldom used, the fold block should be practiced occasionally just in case it is needed. In the fold block, the lineman to the outside will block the first lineman to his inside, and the lineman to the inside will come around this block (fold) and block the first linebacker to the inside. A reverse fold block is used by the power tackle and quick tackle on 4 hole blocking, with the quick tackle blocking out and the power tackle coming around and blocking the linebacker. This block is shown in Diagram 2-12.

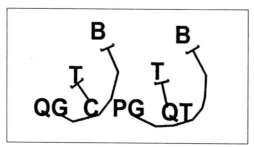

Diagram 2-12. Fold block

Trap Block

The trap block is important because it is used on most running plays. The blocker must use the shoulder that is the same as the direction of his trap, i.e., right shoulder going to the right and left shoulder going to the left. It is important that the trapper goes into the line and anticipates blocking the defender where he originally aligned, because this trap is the toughest. The trapper must be under control, getting an inside-out position on the defender. The trapper must stay on his feet, hitting on the rise, and maintain contact. A trap block is illustrated in Diagram 2-13.

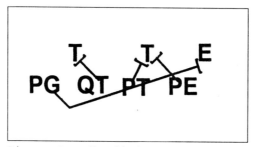

Diagram 2-13. Trap block

Head-Up-Gap Rule

Most well-coached defensive teams will not allow an offensive lineman to release inside on a linebacker, even if a good rip technique is used to try and get inside. Even if the lineman does get through to the linebacker, the defensive lineman will have closed down, making the trap block very difficult. Due to this fact, a head-up-gap rule is necessary. This rule tells the man at the point of attack that if his rule is to block the first man to the inside, and he has a lineman head-up or in his inside gap, he will block the first man to his outside. Most of the time, he will show pass blocking first before blocking the man to his outside. This rule is shown in Diagram 2-14.

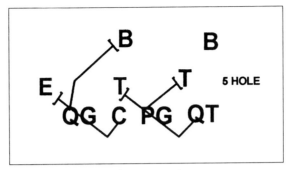

Diagram 2-14. Head-up-gap rule

"Red" Call

This call is made by the quick guard on the 6 hole and the center on the 5 hole to the quick tackle, if they are applying the head-up-gap rule, to alert the quick tackle that his trap will be short and to be ready for a quick trap. This call is shown in Diagram 2-15.

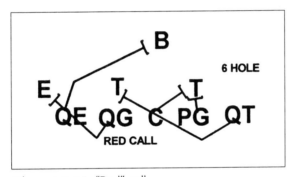

Diagram 2-15. "Red" call

"Switch" Call

When teams are keying the 1 back, a "switch" call is a good change-up call. The power guard will pull and block at the 1 hole, while the quick tackle, power tackle, and power end will block the first man to their inside. The 1 back will block the first man past the power guard toward the center. This call is shown in Diagram 2-16.

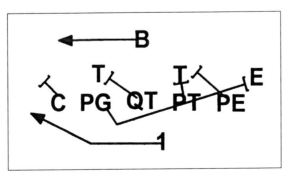

Diagram 2-16. "Switch" call

"Check" Call

This call is made by the power guard in some pass blocking situations. If the power guard makes the call, it must be echoed by the quick tackle, power tackle, and either the power end or 1 back. The power guard makes the call when the fifth defensive man from the outside shoulder of the quick end is in his inside gap or head-up on him. This call changes the blocks for the quick tackle, power tackle, and either the power end or 1 back to the first man to the inside, as shown in Diagram 2-17.

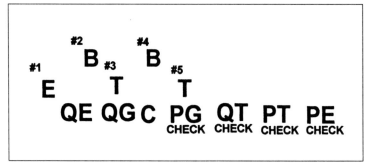

Diagram 2-17. "Check" call

Run Blocking Assignments

Many different ways exist to give linemen their blocking assignments as individual coaches exist. Some coaches give assignments by play, others by numbering the defense, and others by applying a specific rule. In the single wing run blocking schemes described in this book, the linemen get their assignments by what hole the play is going to be run through. For example, on plays 241 and 441, the linemen have the same blocking responsibilities. This method makes it easier for them to remember their assignments, and, if a new play is added, no new learning is added for the linemen. Although 8 holes exist, most of the linemen only have a few responsibilities to learn because their responsibility on one hole is repeated on another hole. Following are the run responsibilities for each line position.

Quick End

- 1 hole: The quick end should pull and lead through the 1 hole looking for the safety. On a "rock" call, the end should look inside for the linebacker first, then for the safety. If split, the end shouldn't lead through the 1 hole, just block the man covering him.

- 2 hole: The quick end should pull and lead through the 2 hole, looking for the corner. On a "rock" call, the end should look inside for the linebacker first, then for the corner. If split, the end shouldn't lead through the 2 hole, just block the man covering him.

- 3 and 4 holes: The quick end should block the playside safety.

- 5 and 6 holes: The quick end should block the first linebacker to the inside away from the hole. If split, the end should block the man covering him.
- 7 hole: The quick end should block the first man to the inside, with possibly a combo with the quick guard.
- 8 hole: The quick end block the second man from head-up to outside, usually the corner.

Quick Guard

- 1, 2, 3, and 4 holes: The quick guard should block the first linebacker from head-up on the center to the backside. The guard may pull around the center to block the linebacker. If the linebacker is gone, continue on to the safety. If a lineman is in the gap between the quick guard and the center, he must combo this man with the center to the linebacker.
- 5 hole: The quick guard should block the second man from the outside shoulder of the quick end to the inside, usually the corner. He should release inside the first man head-up to outside the quick end. If the quick end is split, the guard should block the first linebacker over to inside.
- 6 hole: The quick guard should block the first lineman to the inside (head-up-gap rule).
- 7 and 8 hole: The guard should block the first lineman from head-up on the center to the outside. On 8 hole, the guard should give the "gap" call to the 1 back, if a lineman is head-up on the center to the quick guard's inside gap and a lineman in his outside gap.

Center

- 1, 2, 3, 4, 7, and 8 holes: The center should block the first lineman to the backside or away from the point of attack.
- 5 hole: The center should block the first man toward the power guard (head-up-gap rule).
- 6 hole: The center should block the first lineman from head-up on the center to the power guard.

Power Guard

- 1 and 2 holes: The power guard should call "me" or "you."
- 3 and 4 holes: The power guard should block the first lineman from head-up on the center to the outside. If no lineman is in this position, the guard should block the most dangerous linebacker.
- 5 and 6 holes: The power guard should block the first man from inside gap to the outside.

- 7 and 8 holes: The power guard should block the first linebacker from head-up on the center to the backside. He may pull around the center to get the linebacker. If the linebacker is gone, the guard should block the most dangerous defender. If a lineman is in the gap between him and the center, the power guard must combo this man with the center to the linebacker.

Quick Tackle

- 1 and 2 holes: The quick tackle should call "gap," "me," or "you."
- 3 hole: The quick tackle should block the first lineman from head-up on him to the inside.
- 4 hole: The quick tackle should block the first lineman to the outside.
- 5 hole: The quick tackle should trap the first lineman past the power guard.
- 6 hole: The quick tackle should trap the first lineman past the center.
- 7 and 8 holes: The quick tackle should block the first man from his inside gap to the outside.

Power Tackle

- 1 and 2 holes: The power tackle should call "gap," "me," or "rock."
- 3 hole: The power tackle should block the first man to the inside. He should apply only the head-up part of the head-up-gap rule.
- 4 hole: The power tackle should block the first linebacker head-up to the inside. He may fold with the quick tackle.
- 5 and 6 holes: The power tackle should block the first lineman from past the quick tackle to the outside.
- 7 and 8 holes: The power tackle should block the first man from past the quick tackle to the outside.

Power End

- 1 and 2 holes: The power end should block the first man to the inside.
- 3 hole: The power end should block the first linebacker to the inside.
- 4 and 5 holes: The power end should block the first man from head-up on him to the outside. On 444 power, the end should block the first linebacker to the inside.
- 6 hole: The power end should block the middle safety.
- 7 hole: The power end should pull, lead through the 7 hole, and block the corner.
- 8 hole: The power end should block the middle safety.

The simplicity of these blocking assignments is a strength of the single wing offense. The linemen don't have a lot to learn and can spend their time working on their techniques. As will be seen in following chapters, none of the linemen are asked to perform a block that an average player can't execute.

Pass Blocking Assignments

Quick End

The quick end should block the first man from his outside shoulder to the inside, on any pass that he is not a receiver.

Quick Guard

The quick guard should block the second man from the outside shoulder of the quick end to the inside.

Center

The center should block the third man from the outside shoulder of the quick end to the inside. This block is usually a combo block with either the power guard or quick guard.

Power Guard

The power guard should block the fourth man from the outside shoulder of the quick end to the inside. He should give a "check" call if the fifth man from the outside shoulder of the quick end is in his inside gap or head-up on him.

Quick Tackle

The quick tackle should block the first man past the power guard to the outside. On a "check" call, he should block the first man to the inside.

Power Tackle

The power tackle should block the second man past the power guard to the outside. On a "check" call, he should block the first man to the inside.

Power End

The power end should block the third man past the power guard on any pass that he is not a receiver. On a check call, the end should block the first man to the inside.

3

Backfield Play

The Spin

Since the main play series in the single wing offense described in this book is the spinner series, beginning by explaining the spin technique is advisable. Quite a bit of information in old coaching magazines and older books written about the single wing actually exists on how to perform the spin technique. The only problem with these texts is that the spin technique is described as very complicated so that the quarterback, or fullback in other single wing offenses, would seemingly have to be the world's greatest athlete. When teaching younger players the spin, just snap the ball to the quarterback and have him spin. Although this technique appears too simple, the coach shouldn't want the player so concerned with the spin that he impedes his natural athletic ability. After the player feels comfortable receiving the snap and spinning, the coach can give some coaching points if the player needs some fine-tuning. The spin isn't actually a spin, but a series of small steps that allow the player to rotate 360 degrees in a small area, remaining in enough control to come out of the spin being able to explode into the line of scrimmage. On his first step, the quarterback should be going slightly toward the line of scrimmage to help with the mesh of the tailback. The quarterback takes the first step with his inside leg, and, as he sets this foot down, that foot should be parallel to the line of scrimmage. This positioning will make the rest of the spin easier. Also, the quarterback should bring the ball into his body upon receiving the snap to help in hiding the ball. The second step is with the outside foot. How far the quarterback steps depends on where he is going after he comes out of the spin. The first step is with the toes pointing at 12 o'clock. The second step will be at approximately 2 o'clock when going to the 3 hole, 12 o'clock when going to the 5 hole, and 11 o'clock when going to the 6 hole. The third step is a logical progression of stepping to the appropriate hole. These steps are illustrated in Diagrams 3-1 through 3-4.

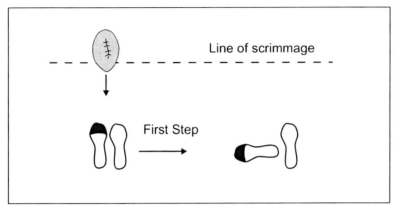

Diagram 3-1. First step

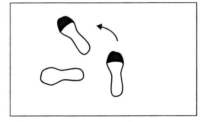

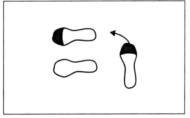

Diagram 3-2. Second step at 2 o'clock when going to the 3 hole

Diagram 3-3. Second step at 12 o'clock when going to the 5 hole

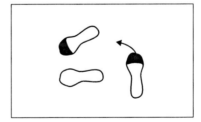

Diagram 3-4. Second step at 11 o'clock when going to the 6 hole

As mentioned under center play, the snap is very important for the spin to be successful. It must be accurate and low (between the knee and thigh). This position allows the quarterback to conceal the ball and fake, which momentarily freezes the defense because they don't know who has the ball or where the point of attack is going to be. This technique is a must for the spin series to be effective.

Faking

For the spin series to work, each of the backs must fake as if they are carrying the ball. The quarterback doesn't stick the ball into the belly of the tailback or wingback as they go past him. These backs have the responsibility to fake like they have received the ball. The back will tuck and have his arms as if he received the ball. The backs should fake well past the line of scrimmage. The backs should have their arms in such a manner, looking like they have the ball. When carrying the ball, the back will have both hands on the ball, with each hand covering a point of the ball. The ball will stay covered until he has passed the last defensive player. The faking backs should also have their arms in this manner. Keeping their arms a ball distance away from their body is important in faking. This positioning makes the fake much more realistic. The coach can illustrate this technique by placing a ball in the player's stomach, having him tuck it away as if he were carrying it, then taking the ball out so the player will know how far away from his body his arms should be. When carrying the ball or faking, the backs should have their forearms touching so that the ball is not visible. Also, the faking backs should run hard as if they had the ball. The faking backs can be taught to run into the last man on the line of scrimmage to the side that they are faking, hit and spin off him and continue up the field. This technique makes the fake that much more effective. Faking in the spin series is critical to success. Sometimes, players will tend to slack off on carrying out their fakes during practice. The coach cannot let players be lax. The coach can point out in film study how a good fake produces a big play and how a poor fake ruined a play. A drill that can be used with the backs is for the players to run a play without the coach knowing what play it is, forcing the coach to see if he can find the ball. When the backs can fool the coach, they are faking as they should.

Handoffs

When the ball is handed off is also important in the spin series. When the tailback is going to carry the ball, he should receive it when the quarterback has his back to the side that the tailback is going toward. For the defenders to the playside to see the ball being handed off is almost impossible. The tailback and quarterback must be close together for the mesh of the handoff. If the ball is stuck out for the tailback, the deception on the play is ruined. As he receives the ball, the tailback must bend his upper body, keep his forearms together as he secures the ball with both hands, and run to the hole. He will keep the ball covered until he passes the last defensive player. When the wingback is going to carry the ball, the quarterback will be about three-quarters of the way through his spin and will have his back to the side that the wingback is running toward. Again, the quarterback and the wingback must achieve a close mesh for the handoff. The wingback uses the same technique as the tailback when receiving the ball. When the quarterback is carrying the ball, he immediately secures the ball with both hands after receiving the snap, completes his spin, and runs to the hole. The tailback and wingback are responsible for faking as they pass the quarterback. Again, the mesh must be close, and the backs must make it look like they have the ball. The fact that the quarterback's back is to the side that the faking back is going toward makes this easier.

Timing is important in the spin series. The tailback, wingback, and quarterback must work on timing until they become a well-tooled machine. The tailback must not cut too soon after passing the quarterback so that he doesn't collide with the wingback. The wingback must aim at the hip of the quarterback so that he doesn't interfere with the path of the tailback. With practice, these maneuvers become routine.

Backfield Run Blocking Assignments

With the exception of the blocking back, the backs do not have many blocking assignments. However, even though blocks are few, these blocks are usually crucial to the success of the play.

Blocking Back

- 1 and 2 holes: The blocking back should block the first linebacker head-up to outside the power guard. On a "rock" call, he should block at the point of attack instead of the linebacker. On a "switch" call, the back should block the first man from the power guard toward the center.
- 3 hole: The blocking back should block the first lineman head-up to outside the power tackle.
- 4 hole: The blocking back should block the first lineman head-up to inside the quick tackle.
- 5 and 6 holes: The blocking back should block the first man past the power guard to the outside.
- 7 hole: The blocking back should block the first man head-up to outside the quick end.
- 8 hole: The blocking back should block the first linebacker inside of the quick end. On a "gap" call, the back should block the first lineman head-up to outside the quick guard.

Quarterback

- 1 hole: The quarterback should lead block on power, carry or fake on others.
- 2 hole: The quarterback should lead block on power, carry or fake on others.
- 3 hole: The quarterback should lead block on power, carry or fake on others.

- 4 hole: The quarterback should block the first man outside power tackle on 444 power, block first man outside of quick guard on 444 motion, and carry or fake on others.
- 5 hole: The quarterback should fake or carry.
- 6 hole: The quarterback should fake or carry.
- 7 hole: The quarterback should fake or carry.
- 8 hole: The quarterback should block the first man outside of quick guard on 438 motion, carry or fake on others.

Wingback

- 1 hole: The wingback should block the first man to the inside.
- 2 hole: The wingback should block safety, fake or carry on others.
- 3 hole: The wingback should block safety, fake or carry on others.
- 4 hole: The wingback should block safety on power, fake or carry on others.
- 5 hole: The wingback should fake or carry.
- 6 hole: The wingback should block safety, fake or carry on others.
- 7 hole: The wingback should fake or carry.
- 8 hole: The wingback should block on 228 and 248, fake or carry on others.

Tailback

- 1 hole: The tailback should fake or carry.
- 2 hole: The tailback should fake or carry.
- 3 hole: The tailback should fake or carry.
- 4 hole: The tailback should block on 224 motion, fake or carry on others.
- 5 hole: The tailback should fake or carry.
- 6 hole: The tailback should fake or carry.
- 7 hole: The tailback should block on 227, fake or carry on others.
- 8 hole: The tailback should block on 238 motion, 238 option, and 228, fake or carry on others.

Pass Blocking Responsibility

As with run blocking, the backs do not have a lot of pass blocking responsibility. Also true, however, is that their blocks are extremely important to the success of the play.

Blocking Back

On passes that the blocking back blocks to the power end's side, he should block the third man past the power guard's block. On a "check" call, the back should block the first man head-up to outside the power tackle. On passes that the blocking back blocks to the quick end's side, the back should block the first man outside the quick guard's block. On other passes, the back should run his assigned route.

Quarterback

On pass 241, the quarterback should pick up the quick end's man. On 441 power pass and pass 441, the quarterback should block the power end's man. On others, he should pass or run his assigned route.

Wingback

On pass 223, the wingback should block with the quick end. On others, he should run his assigned route.

Tailback

On passes the tailback blocks to the quick end's side, he should block the first man outside of the quick guard's block. On passes the tailback blocks to the power end's side, he should block the third man past the power guard.

4

The Spin Series

Because of its deception, the spin series is the basic play series in the single wing offense that is run at Ithaca (MI) High School. Most of the single wing series offer some deception, but the spin series is the ultimate in deception. The toughest defensive players to block are the linebackers. The spin series forces the linebackers to hesitate while trying to read the play, thus allowing the offensive blockers to get the position necessary to block them. Another advantage of the spin series is that it can be successful with backs that have less than blazing speed. Due to the misdirection of the spin series action and deception caused by faking, a back with average speed can often get big gains because the defense doesn't know who has the ball.

Following are diagrams of the spin series plays against the most common defenses and the coaching points important for the success of the play. The blocking responsibilities for each of the holes have already been discussed in Chapters 2 and 3.

Coaching Points for Play 241

Every offense must have one play that can be run no matter what the defense. Play 241 is that play in the single wing offense. The line calls allow this play to be run against any defensive front, and the blocking assignments account for the linebackers and secondary. As with all of the spinner plays, a good, low snap insures the deception needed to hold the linebackers. In all of the spin series, the snap should be directed at the inside knee of the quarterback. The tailback and quarterback should be close on the exchange, as distance destroys fakes and causes fumbles. The wing's block is key. The wing should stop penetration and maintain his block for the play to be successful. The tailback will run off this block. The line should stop penetration with good cutoff blocks to allow the quick end to get to his block. The blocking back picking up the linebacker whether he blitzes or flows to the ball is also important, unless it is a "rock" call. The play can be run with the quarterback faking into the line or faking his bootleg. The bootleg fake is usually better, because it holds the backside defensive players and also sets up the bootleg pass.

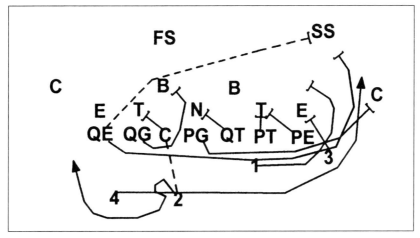

Diagram 4-1. Play 241 versus 5-2-4

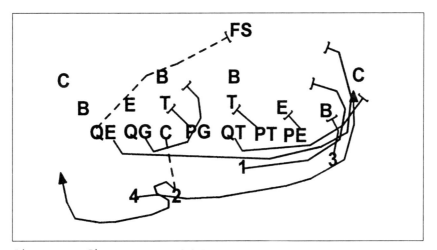

Diagram 4-2. Play 241 versus 6-2-3

Coaching Points for Play 241-Read

Play 241-read is good to run against eight-man fronts. The wing's block usually isn't needed, and he can be used to add to the deception in the backfield. The power end's rule is different, but he usually winds up blocking the same man that he would on 241 against an eight-man front. All of the keys for 241 carry over for 241-read. The low snap, the closeness of the backs, including the wingback, the blocking back's block on the linebacker, and the good cutoff blocks are all important for the success of the play. As in play 241, the quarterback can either fake into the line or fake his bootleg action. The tailback will run off the block of the power end. Against a seven-man front, it could be either in or out, depending on the block of the power end. It is almost always out against eight-man fronts. As with 241, this play can be run against any defense.

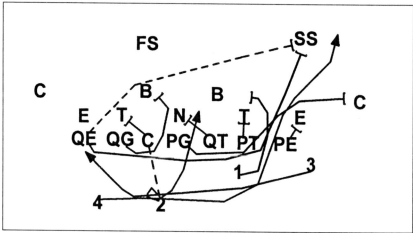

Diagram 4-3. Play 241-read versus 5-2-4

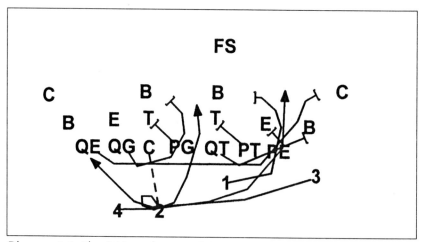

Diagram 4-4. Play 241-read versus 6-2-3

Coaching Points for Play 223

Again, the low snap is key for good fakes to take place. The quarterback will put the ball away immediately upon receiving the snap as he starts his spin. The tailback and wingback must be close to the quarterback and are responsible for carrying out excellent fakes. They should fake toward the last man on the line of scrimmage, bounce off them as if they had the ball, and then continue to carry out their fakes downfield. Their fakes will usually determine the success of the play. The quarterback should know where the double-team block will take place and run off that block. This play is run many times from an over formation so that the blocking back has a running start for his block. The power end's block on the linebacker is a simple one, but very important for the success of the play.

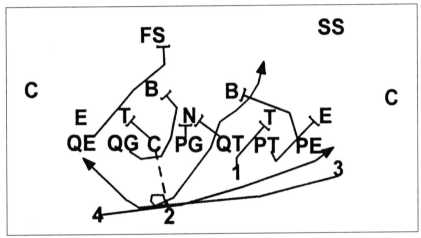

Diagram 4-5. Play 223 versus 5-2-4

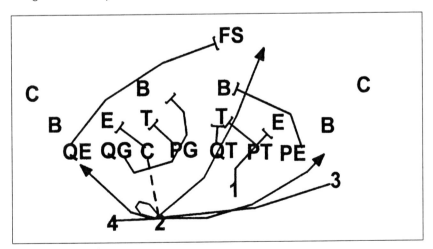

Diagram 4-6. Play 223 versus 6-2-3

Coaching Points for Play 225

Most of the keys for play 223 to be successful also carry over for play 225. The low snap, good fakes, etc., are important for the success of the play. The blocking back may change his alignment to the outside of the quick tackle, allowing both players to carry out their assignments easier. This play is good against teams that are keying the blocking back as he goes away from the hole. The quick end's block on the linebacker is simple, but key to the success of the play. The quick guard should release inside the last man on the line of scrimmage on his way to block the corner, so that this man can't crash down into the play. If the quick end is split, the quick guard will block the linebacker, and the quick end will block the corner. The quarterback should be aware of the quick tackle's trap block, so that he can run off of this block.

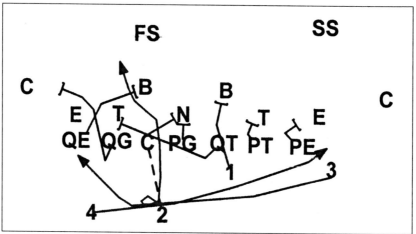

Diagram 4-7. Play 225 versus 5-2-4

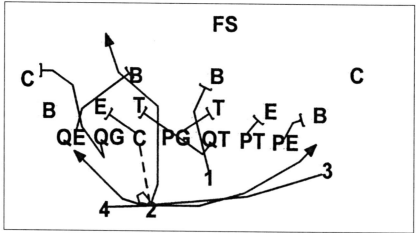

Diagram 4-8. Play 225 versus 6-2-3

Coaching Points for Play 235

Most of the coaching points for 235 are the same as 225 because the play is hitting the same hole. Play 235 usually has the best average in yards gained. This play involves an inside handoff. It hits extremely quick and away from the flow of the backs, including the blocking back. Timing is very important on the play, with each wingback doing it differently, depending upon his speed. The important thing is that he must reach the handoff point at the correct time for the play to run smoothly. The quarterback and wingback should work on this timing until perfect. It is also important that the wingback break to the sideline after he gets past the quick tackle's trap block.

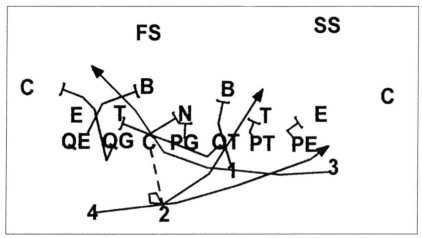

Diagram 4-9. Play 235 versus 5-2-4

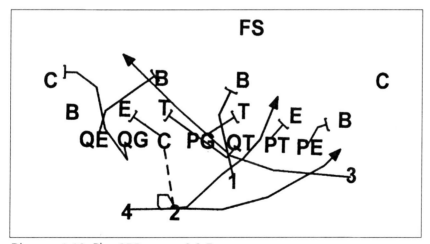

Diagram 4-10. Play 235 versus 6-2-3

Coaching Points for Play 226

The coaching points for 226 are the same as for 225. Either 226 or 225 will be run during a game, depending upon how the defense is aligning. If running to the 6 hole, run play 235 with 226 blocking by calling the play 236. This change will not hurt the timing of the play because the hole is near the same place because of the defensive alignment.

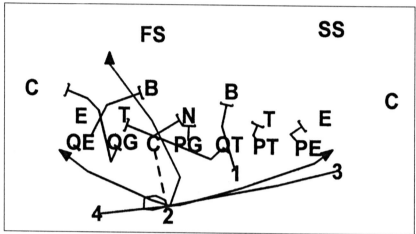

Diagram 4-11. Play 226 versus 5-2-4

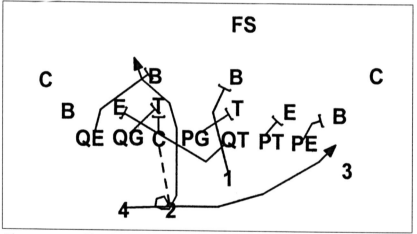

Diagram 4-12. Play 226 versus 6-2-3

Coaching Points for Play 237

This play is similar to 235 as far as the timing is concerned. This play is run with an inside handoff because the wingback doesn't have a sharp cut to hit the hole, and he gets to the hole quicker. The timing between the back getting to the hole and the blocks at the hole are better with the inside handoff. It is important that the tailback has a good fake and runs into the last man on the line of scrimmage, so that the defender can't chase down the play from behind. The quick guard and quick end have key blocks on the play, especially if they are one-on-one blocks. They cannot allow penetration by the defense. If possible, the quick end should try to bounce to the linebacker with a double-team block. The power end's block will usually determine whether it is a big play or not. He has to hustle to the hole, but the play will pick up big yardage if he gets there quickly.

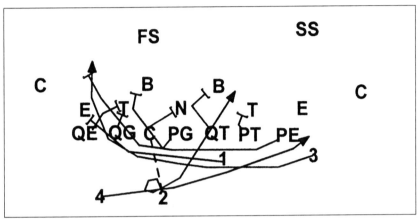

Diagram 4-13. Play 237 versus 5-2-4

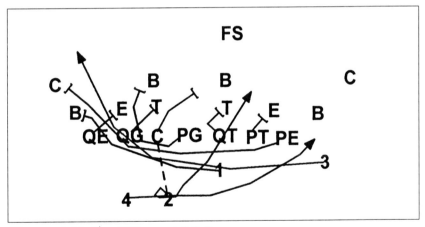

Diagram 4-14. Play 237 versus 6-2-3

These seven spin series plays are the heart of this run offense. At the lower levels, this series may be all of the run offense that a team learns. At the varsity level, the offense must master the spin series before any other series are introduced.

5

The Power Series

Many teams that run the single wing use the power series as their primary run offense. It is the series that most people think of when they hear single wing football. It is, in many coaches' opinions, the best series of power plays in football. Adding one more blocker to the best power plays in any T series creates the single wing power series. It is used as a change-up series to the spin series. The power series is easier to teach than the spin series because it doesn't require the timing of the spin series. For this reason, it can be installed quickly. For the most part, the blocking is exactly the same, so the line doesn't have any new techniques to learn. The power series is very effective versus teams that like to sit and read. Also, in short yardage situations, the power series is very effective in picking up the first down. The one drawback of the power series is that most of the plays give the defense a fast flow read, because no deception is involved. The flow of the backs tells the defense immediately the direction of the play. Since the flow is telling, the blocks are a little more difficult, except at the hole because of the extra blocker. An advantage of the power series is that the counters and reverses are very effective due to the same fast flow read. When the defense sells out on the initial flow of the backs to stop the base plays, they are set up for the blocks that make the counters and reverses successful. It could be argued that the counters and reverses from the power series are more effective than they are from the spin series. All in all, the power series is a very good series to complement the spin series.

Following are diagrams of the power series plays against the most common defenses and the coaching points that are important for the success of the play. The blocking responsibilities for each of the holes have already been discussed in Chapters 2 and 3.

Coaching Points for Play 441

As in the spin series, a good snap is a must. The difference in the snap between the two series is the snap direction. In the spin series, the snap is directed at the inside knee of the quarterback. In the power series, the snap is usually almost straight back, so that the back can be moving in the direction of the play as he receives the snap. The coaching points for 1 hole blocking for play 241 are also true for 441. The biggest difference is that 441 has an extra blocker. The quarterback now leads the play and will block the most dangerous defender. The scouting report will usually determine who the quarterback should block. For example, if the opponent has an outstanding outside linebacker, the quarterback will look to see if the wing needs help with his block and help him if he does. The defense's outstanding player could be the corner, the inside linebacker, or another player. The point is that the quarterback is available as an extra blocker to help out where needed or to lead the play and pick up the most dangerous defender. Play 441 is a fast flow play, so everyone, especially pulling linemen, must get off the ball quickly and maintain their blocks. The tailback runs off the wing's block, as he does in 241, but must also be aware of the quarterback's block.

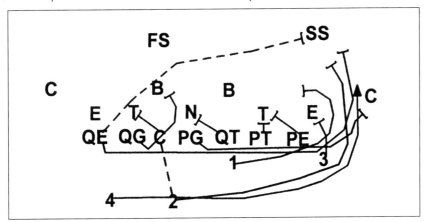

Diagram 5-1. Play 441 versus 5-2-4

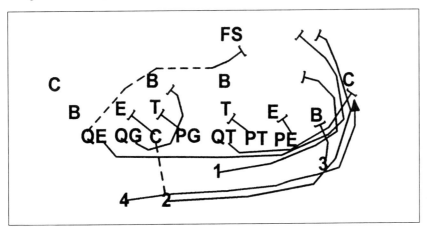

Diagram 5-2. Play 441 versus 6-2-3

Coaching Points for Play 442

This power series play corresponds with 241-read in the spin series. It is especially effective against eight-man fronts. As in 241-read, the wing is used for deception, whereas in 442 the wing is used as an extra blocker. The tailback must make the play look like 441 to aid in the blocking. As in most of the power series plays, the quarterback is an extra blocker that can be used wherever he is needed. The power end's block is important. If he can bounce to the linebacker, versus most seven-man fronts, it may help in getting a big play. However, he should be sure that the power tackle doesn't need his help on a double team first. Versus eight-man fronts, his down block can't allow penetration. Against some teams, the power end is a good man to have the quarterback help out on. Play 442 is also a fast flow play, so everyone must really get off on the snap.

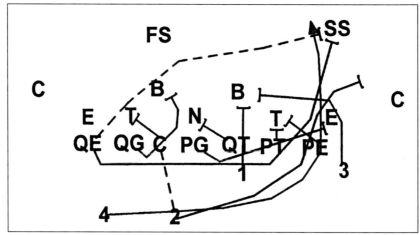

Diagram 5-3. Play 442 versus 5-2-4

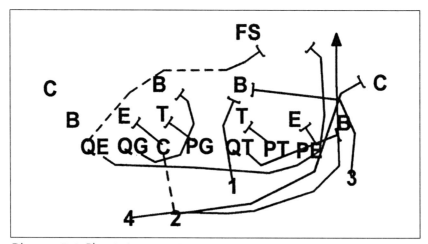

Diagram 5-4. Play 442 versus 6-2-3

Coaching Points for Plays 443 and 444 Power

These two plays are discussed together because the coaching points for both plays are very similar. These plays are usually used in short-yardage situations, but can be used in any situation. The blocking back's block is key on both plays. He may adjust his alignment to get the best blocking angle possible. At worst, he must get a stalemate with the defender he is blocking for the play to be successful. The tailback must make the play look like 441, if running it in a normal down and distance situation. However, if it is a short-yardage situation, the tailback will explode right into the hole to get the necessary yardage. In both cases, the tailback must know where the double-teams are taking place, so that he can run off them. The quarterback leads on 443 the same as he does on 441 and 442, blocking the most dangerous defender or helping out with

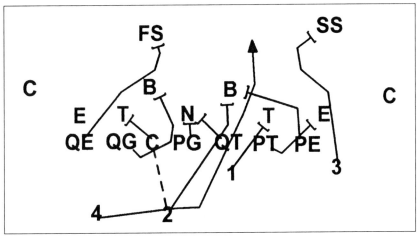

Diagram 5-5. Play 443 versus 5-2-4

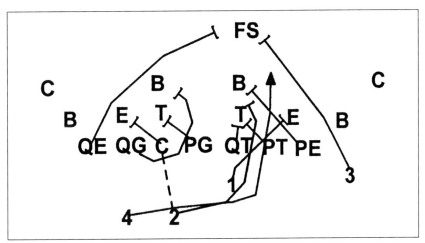

Diagram 5-6. Play 443 versus 6-2-3

a particular man. On 444 power, the quarterback must block the first man outside of the power tackle and not allow any penetration. This block is key, especially in short yardage with the tailback going directly into the hole, because a good defensive player can break up the play if he is allowed to penetrate into the backfield. The toughest block is the quick guard's block on the backside linebacker. Either the blocking back or possibly the quarterback can help on this defender if the quick guard cannot get him alone. These plays hit quickly, so the wingback and quick end need to get their downfield blocks quickly for a big play to result.

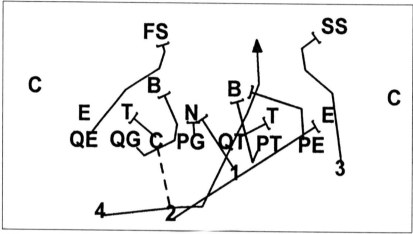

Diagram 5-7. Play 444 power versus 5-2-4

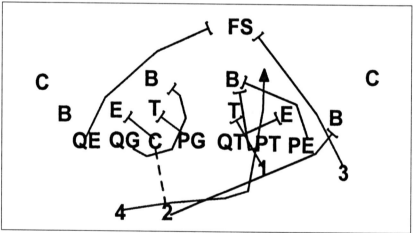

Diagram 5-8. Play 444 power versus 6-2-4

Coaching Points for Play 435

All of the coaching points for play 235 pertain to play 435. Being an inside handoff, the timing on the play is critical. This play hits slightly quicker than 235, so the wing doesn't need to delay. Different wings may have to use different steps to make it run smooth. This play is good to take advantage of a backside linebacker that is really flying to the strongside.

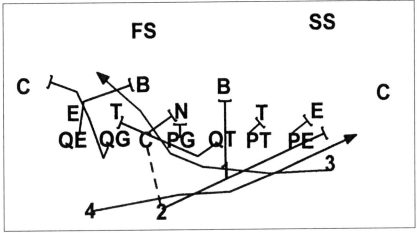

Diagram 5-9. Play 435 versus 5-2-4

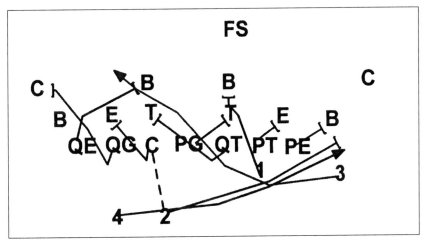

Diagram 5-10. Play 435 versus 6-2-3

Coaching Points For Play 416

This single wing play is innovative. The play comes off 444 power action and takes advantage of an aggressive backside linebacker. The blocking back must take a jab or hesitation step and takes an inside handoff from the tailback. He will run off the trap block of the quick tackle and aim for the sideline. The tailback and the blocking back should be close for a good fake. After the handoff, the tailback must continue into the line and carry out his fake.

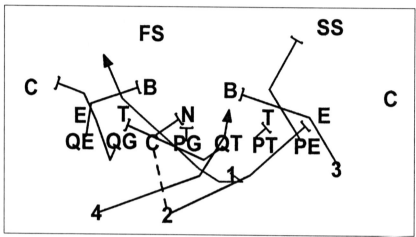

Diagram 5-11. Play 416 versus 5-2-4

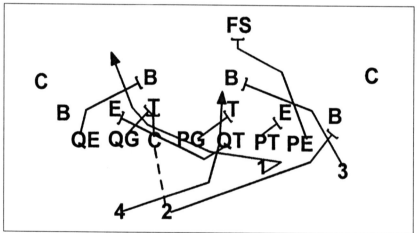

Diagram 5-12. Play 416 versus 6-2-3

Coaching Points for Play 437

Like plays 435 and 416, this play takes advantage of over-aggressive backside pursuit. Play 437 hits a little slower than 435 or 416, but is still a very effective play. The quarterback's block on the last man on the line of scrimmage is key so that that man is occupied and can't chase the play. As on all 7 hole plays, the blocks of the quick guard and quick end are very important to the success of the play, especially when they are one-on-one blocks. The power end's block on the corner may determine if it is a big play or not. Trey is a good formation to run this play from because of the usual defensive adjustment made to the trey formation, especially if the offense has successfully run play 441 from this formation. Another good play is 437-keep, which is actually 441, with a fake to the wingback and everyone else 1 hole blocking. The offense should run 437 a few times and then run 437-keep.

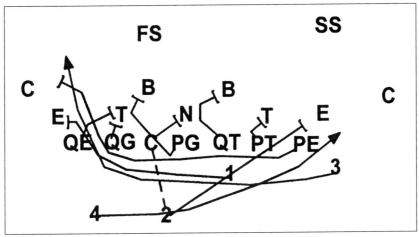

Diagram 5-13. Play 437 versus 5-2-4

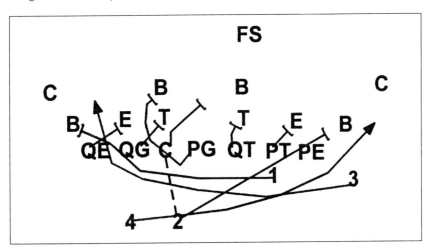

Diagram 5-14. Play 437 versus 6-2-3

These seven power series plays are very easy to install, because the line doesn't have to learn any new techniques and the backs' new learning is minimal. The power series offers a good change of pace to the spin series and forces more preparation on the defense.

6

The Motion Series

The third series installed in the single wing offense should be the motion series. This series puts immediate pressure on the quickside. Each play begins with the wing going in motion toward the quickside as fast as he can. The ball is snapped soon after the wing begins his motion, which is usually the second or third step, depending on the wing's speed. This timing makes it difficult for the defense to react. The motion series is good against teams that overload the powerside or teams that don't adjust to the motion. Some teams will make drastic defensive adjustments when motion is shown. Against these teams, the offense can put the wing in motion and then run the spin series or power series. On two motion series plays, the ball is snapped to the quarterback, and, on the others, the ball is snapped to the tailback.

Coaching Points for Play 238

The techniques for the quarterback and wingback are very similar to the spin series. Some single wing teams run these plays with a half spin. However, more deception occurs with the full spin, and it is one less technique the players have to learn. As in the spin series, the quarterback and wingback should be close on their fake to produce the deception that is necessary and reduce the chance of fumbles. Also, as in the spin series, a good, low snap is necessary for good fakes. The blocking back's block is easier if he aligns in an over set, although it isn't necessary. If he does align in an over set, the power guard's block on the linebacker becomes important if the linebacker is blitzing, because the blocking back will be moving to get position for his block. The blocking back must listen for the "gap" call from the quick guard. He will get the "gap" call against most eight-man fronts. The tailback's block on the last man on the line of scrimmage is necessary to keep this man from catching the wing from behind. The tailback gets better results if he moves for a position outside of the defensive man before he blocks him. Usually, the defensive man will run into the tailback if he has the correct position. That block is all it takes for the wing to get outside, because he is going full speed when he gets the handoff. If the quick end gets his block on the corner, it usually turns into a race between the wing and the defense to the goal line.

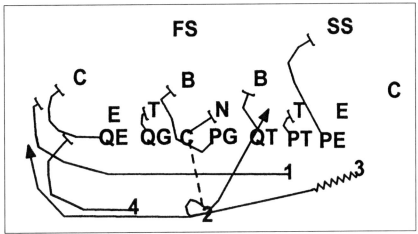

Diagram 6-1. Play 238 versus 5-2-4

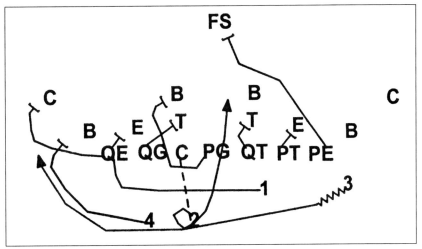

Diagram 6-2. Play 238 versus 6-2-3

Coaching Points for Play 224

Play 224 will usually be successful after running 238 a few times. As with 238, a good fake should occur between the quarterback and wing, which starts with a good low snap. The toughest block on the play is by the quick guard on the backside linebacker. The fake of the wingback sets up this block by the quick guard. All of the coaching points for play 444-power also pertain to this play. The quarterback should run off the block of the quick tackle and then cut upfield looking for the block of the quick end on the safety.

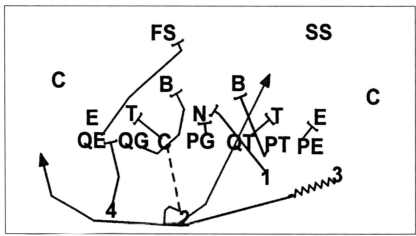

Diagram 6-3. Play 224 versus 5-2-4

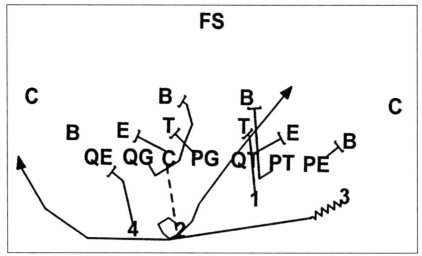

Diagram 6-4. Play 224 versus 6-2-4

Coaching Points for Play 438

Although similar to play 238, play 438 has more deception. Play 438 is usually run against seven-man fronts. The play is difficult to run against some eight-man fronts, because of blocking assignments. The toughest block is for the blocking back to hook the last man on the line of scrimmage, if "gap" isn't called. If a "gap" call is made, the quarterback must fake into this man to keep him from catching the wing from behind. Although play 438 can be run against eight-man fronts, other plays in the motion series would be a better choice. On motion series plays when the ball is snapped to the tailback, the quarterback should cheat back a little. On the snap, he will take a short drop step to allow the wing to run between him and the tailback. Upon receiving the snap, the tailback will spin to his outside. This spin will allow him to have his back to the line for the fakes or handoffs to either the quarterback or wingback.

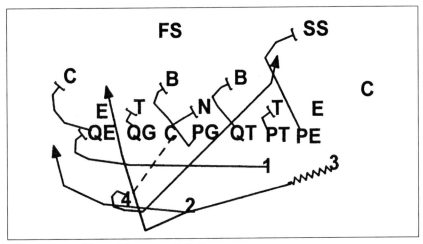

Diagram 6-5. Play 438 versus 5-2-4

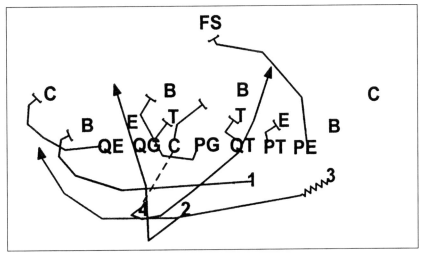

Diagram 6-6. Play 438 versus 6-2-3

Coaching Points for Play 427

This play is very good versus defenses overloaded to the powerside. Good fakes should exist between the backs. The wing and the tailback must carry out their fakes for the play to achieve maximum results. Again, the quarterback will align a little deeper and take his drop step on the snap to allow the wing to go between him and the tailback. The handoff to the quarterback should take place on the outside. This method gives a better fake, and it also gives the power end a better chance to beat the quarterback through the hole to block the corner. This play is good to run when the end man on the line of scrimmage makes it difficult to run 438 or 238. The blocking back has an easy block when he takes himself out of the play chasing the wingback, thus creating a huge hole for the quarterback to run through.

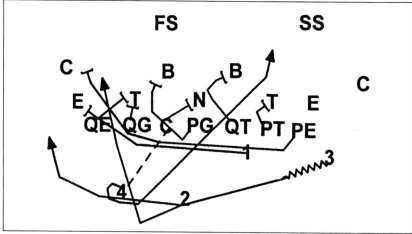

Diagram 6-7. Play 427 versus 5-2-4

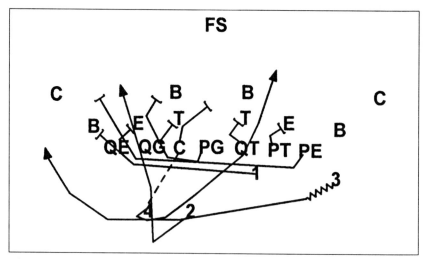

Diagram 6-8. Play 427 versus 6-2-3

Coaching Points for Play 444

The fakes of the wing and the quarterback are important to this play. The tailback should not hurry these fakes. On this play, the quarterback should fake into the last man on the line of scrimmage so that he can't catch the play from behind. All of the coaching points for 444-power also pertain to this play, as they did for play 224. The tailback, as the quarterback did on play 224, should run off the block of the quick tackle, cut straight up field, and look for the block of the quick end on the safety.

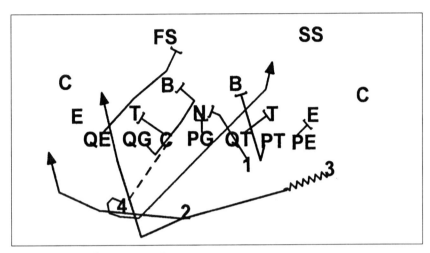

Diagram 6-9. Play 444 motion versus 5-2-4

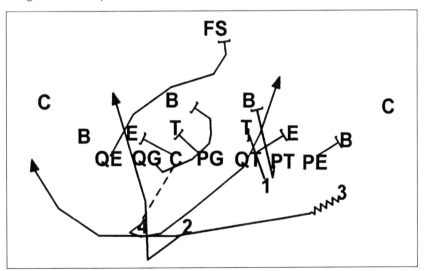

Diagram 6-10. Play 444 motion versus 6-2-3

Coaching Points for Play 224

Although not really a part of the motion series, play 224 comes off of motion series action, thus it is in this section, instead of under supplemental plays. The ball is snapped to the quarterback, who runs through the 4 hole, while the wing and tailback execute their responsibilities of play 444 motion. The quarterback cheats up a little, and the snap is low at his outside knee so he can hit the hole quickly. This play is especially good against teams that have prepared for the motion series. The play hits very quickly and can develop into a big play.

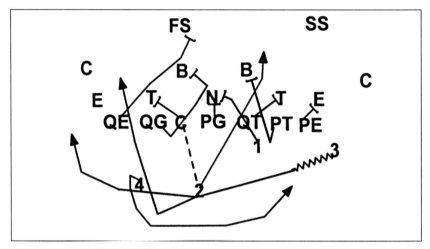

Diagram 6-11. Play 224 dive versus 5-2-4

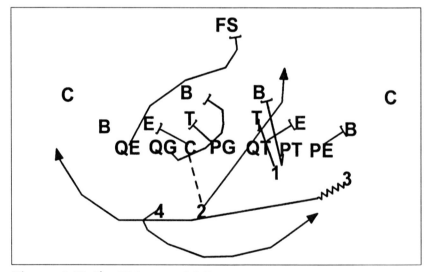

Diagram 6-12. Play 224 versus 6-2-3

7

The Buck Lateral Series

Many single wing advocates believe the buck lateral series is the mainstay of the single wing offense. With the right personnel, it can be a very explosive offensive series. However, following are some reasons that explain why it doesn't fit well with an offense that features the spin series.

The first reason is that, like the spin series, the buck lateral series takes a lot of practice to perfect the timing. A coach should be careful not to try and do too many things with the single wing, or he'll find that he isn't doing any of them very well. Another reason is that the buck lateral series requires personnel placement that is different than the other series. The quarterback (2 back) is usually not a fullback-type player. As mentioned earlier in this book, the quarterback is more of a finesse-type player. He must have good ball handling skills so that he can fake in the spin and motion series, carry occasionally, and have the ability to pass. In the buck lateral series, the quarterback needs to be a big tough runner, as he will be hitting into the interior of the line on many of the plays. The dive or buck plays hit quickly and are a big advantage of this series. However, the success of the buck lateral series is in direct proportion to the ability of the fullback (2 back) to run inside. The other key position in the buck lateral series is the 1 back. For the buck lateral team, the 1 back is their quarterback, and he would have many of the characteristics of the 2 back in the previously described offense. In the spin and motion series, the 1 back is more of a blocker and receiver and not necessarily a very good ball handler. The final reason, and maybe the most important one for not running the buck lateral series with the spin series, is that it would require changes in the blocking for many of the plays, i.e., the 1 back is involved in play faking in the buck lateral plays, not blocking, as in most running plays.

If a coach wanted to make the buck lateral series his base series, he could still run the power series and the motion series successfully. However, for the reasons stated previously, both the spin series and buck lateral series cannot be run successfully together without one taking something away from the other. With that said, following are the base plays and some change-ups for the buck lateral series. Most of the following buck lateral series was learned from Keith Piper, who coached at Dennison University, and has sadly passed away, and Steve Ragsdale, who coaches at Giles High School. Both of these coaches have used the buck lateral with great success.

Coaching Points for Play 223 Buck Lateral

This play hits very fast, but still has deception. As in all single wing plays, the snap is very important. The center should put the ball on the outside knee of the 2 back. It is important that the 2 back doesn't move too quickly on the snap. The 2 back should take a short six-inch step forward with his outside foot so that the timing with the 1 back is correct. The 2 back should catch the ball out in front of him and extend it toward the 1 back with his hands on the back half of the ball. The linebackers should see the ball so that they will hold their positions and can be blocked. This motion serves the same purpose as the spin action in the spin series, except in the spin series the objective is to hide the ball to hold the linebackers. The 1 back takes a 12-inch step to the inside with his inside foot and pivots while keeping a narrow base. The 1 back

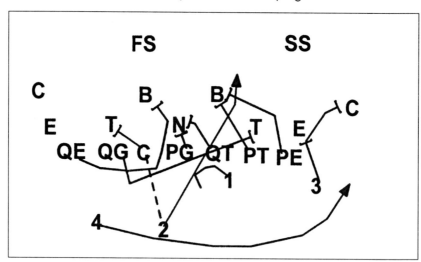

Diagram 7-1. Play 223 buck lateral versus 5-2-4

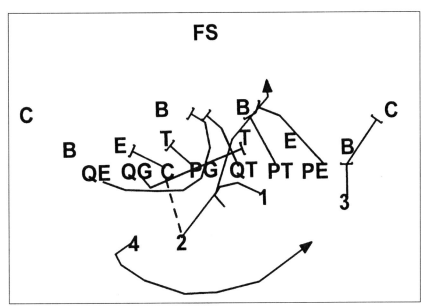

Diagram 7-2. Play 223 buck lateral versus 6-2-3

has his forearms on his hips and his hands in his crotch. A good fake should occur between the 1 back and 2 back. As in the spin series, the two backs must be close together. The shoulder pads of the backs should overlap on their fake, with the inside shoulder pad of the 1 back after his pivot, brushing the outside shoulder pad of the 2 back. The 2 back brings the ball in and covers it, staying as low as possible as he passes the 1 back, then runs off the trap block of the quick guard. After the 2 back has passed, the 1 back must carry out his pitch fake to the 4 back and make the play look as much like 241 buck lateral as possible.

Coaching Points for Play 222 Buck Lateral

This play is very similar to 223 buck lateral with some minor adjustments. On this play, the 1 back will take his 12-inch step with his outside foot instead of his inside foot. The rest of the 1 back's techniques are the same as in 223 buck lateral. The 2 back's techniques are the same as in 223 buck lateral, with the obvious exception that the hole is wider. The 2 back must still run inside of the 1 back to create a good fake. The line can use their red zone blocking rules. The 3 back sets up the block on the end and then bounces to the corner. However, if the quick end is unable to get to the linebacker, switch the blocks between the 3 back and quick end. On the switch, the 3 back will go directly to the linebacker and the quick end will go to the corner.

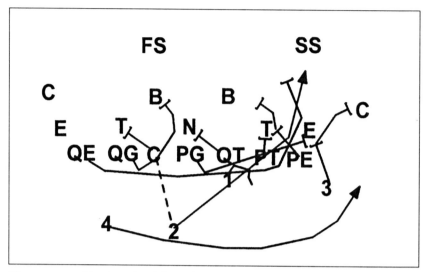

Diagram 7-3. Play 222 buck lateral versus 5-2-4

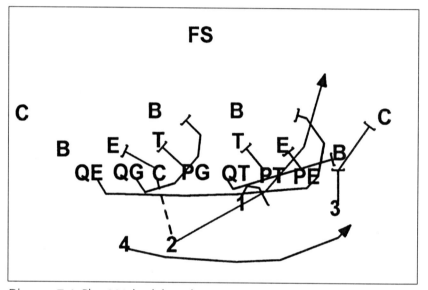

Diagram 7-4. Play 222 buck lateral versus 6-2-3

Coaching Points for Play 226 (225) Buck Lateral

This play is a good cutback against fast flowing linebackers. Use either 5 or 6 hole blocking, depending on how the defense is aligned. The 1 back and 2 back use the same techniques as they do on 223 buck lateral, with the exception that the 2 back will follow the block of the quick guard and run off his trap block in the 5 or 6 hole.

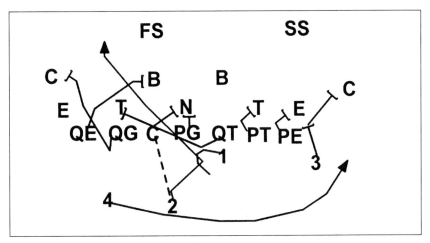

Diagram 7-5. Play 226 (225) buck lateral versus 5-2-4

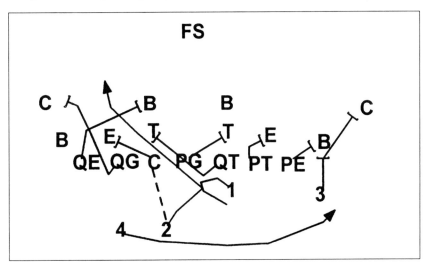

Diagram 7-6. Play 226 (225) buck lateral versus 6-2-3

Coaching Points for Play 235 (236) Buck Lateral

This play is to the buck lateral series as 235 is to the spin series. Anytime that the backside linebacker is making tackles on the frontside against the 223 or 222 buck lateral plays, 235 buck lateral should be successful. The 2 back's technique on this play is the same as on 223 buck lateral, except that he will give the ball to the 1 back. As he approaches the 1 back with the ball extended, he will place the ball into the hands of the 1 back and carry out his fake into the linebacker. Again, the two backs should be close, shoulder pad to shoulder pad, so that the ball is hidden and a good fake can be carried out. Upon receiving the ball, the 1 back will handoff to the 3 back as he goes by and then carry out his pitch fake to the 4 back. The 3 back must take a jab step, as if he were blocking for 241 buck lateral, so the timing of the play will work. The 3 back should go by the 1 back as soon as he can after the 2 back has handed off the ball, but not too quickly so that it is a difficult handoff for the 1 back. Timing is key for the success of the play. After receiving the handoff, the 3 back will follow the block of the quick guard and run off his trap block. Then he should try and get to the outside as quickly as possible.

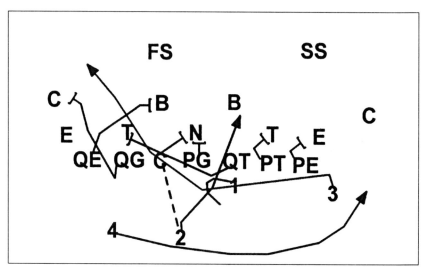

Diagram 7-7. Play 235 (236) buck lateral versus 5-2-4

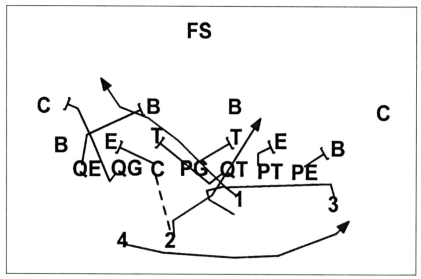

Diagram 7-8. Play 235 (236) buck lateral versus 6-2-3

Coaching Points for Play 241 Buck Lateral

This play is big in the buck lateral series. If the inside plays have been successful, then 241 buck lateral can be a game breaker. The 2 back's technique is the same as in 235 buck lateral. His handoff and fake are very important, and the success of the play depends on them. The 1 back will receive the handoff from the 2 back and pitch from the hip with no step on the pitch. The pitch is all in one motion: one, receive the handoff, two, cock, and three, pitch the ball. It is not a long pitch and should get to the 4 back as quickly as possible. The pulling linemen should try and get outside, in position on the man they are going to block, as this position allows the 4 back to stay outside and not have to make an inside-out move.

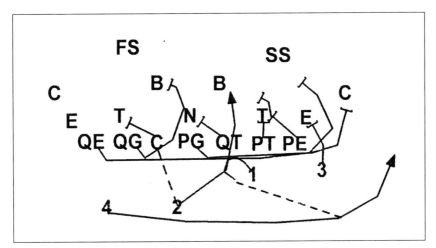

Diagram 7-9. Play 241 buck lateral versus 5-2-4

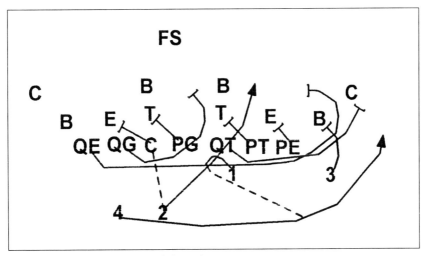

Diagram 7-10. Play 241 buck lateral versus 6-2-3

Coaching Points for Play 241 Buck Lateral Pass

Many passing possibilities exist from the buck lateral series. Teams that use the buck lateral series as their base offense often have the 1 back do the passing, because of the type of player that plays this position. He will receive the handoff from the 2 back, drop back, and pass. Another way to run this play is to have the 4 back pass the ball from the 241 buck lateral action. This pass is very familiar for the 4 back because it is almost the same action as in 241 pass and 441 pass. The 4 back will read the corner. If the corner doesn't cover the 3 back, throw to him. If the corner covers the 3 back, the quick end should be open on his crossing route. Throwback possibilities to the 2 back exist if the 4 back has a strong enough arm.

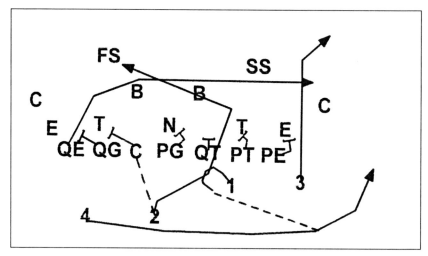

Diagram 7-11. Play 241 buck lateral pass versus 5-2-4

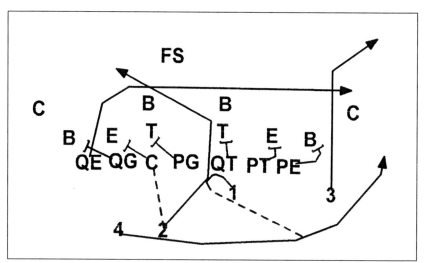

Diagram 7-12. Play 241 buck lateral pass versus 6-2-3

As stated previously, the buck lateral series can be a potent series. The running and passing game can be expanded upon from what has been presented here. But, these plays provide a good beginning place.

8

Supplemental Plays

The spin, power, and motion series make up 99 percent of the single wing running game. However, a few good plays exist that don't fit into any series. These plays take advantage of particular defenses or defensive adjustments to a base offensive formation. Or, it could be defensive adjustment to one of the change-up formations. For whatever reason, these plays can take advantage of defensive adjustments. As a word of caution, the coach should be careful not to add too much. Be sure a sound reason exists for a new play. And, be sure to spend enough time practicing it. Following are some examples of supplemental plays.

Coaching Points for Play 248 Option

Ithaca used to run the option from an unbalanced line to get the look wanted to the shortside, because most teams will adjust and shift to the unbalanced side. This tendency is still true; therefore, run the option to the quickside. It puts a lot of pressure to that side, gets the ball to the best running back, and gets him on the perimeter very quickly. The quarterback should think pitch. He should run downhill at the last man on the line of scrimmage and pitch the ball to the tailback, unless that man goes directly to the tailback. This play is easy to run and can be run from a lot of different formations.

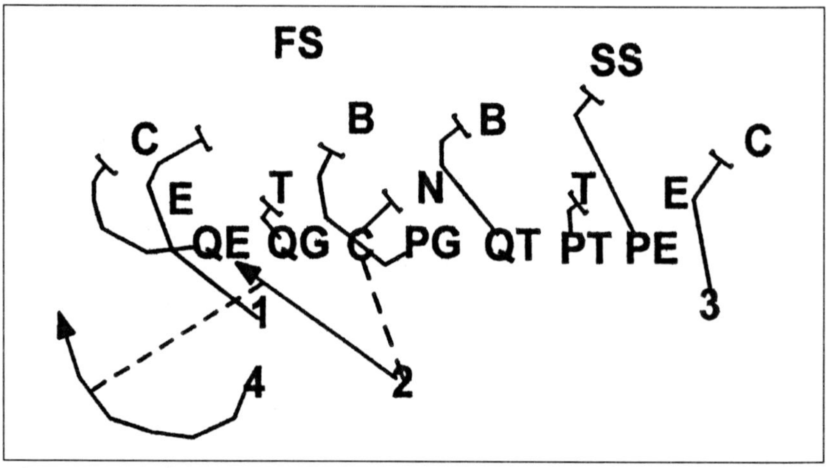

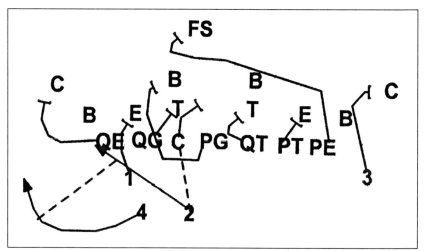

Diagram 8-1. Play 248 option versus 5-2-4

Diagram 8-2. Play 248 option versus 6-2-3

Coaching Points for Play 238 Option

This play must be run from a formation that can have the wing go in motion. Like the power series, this play provides an extra blocker, in this case the tailback. The technique for the quarterback is the same as on play 248. The tailback leads the play and blocks the most dangerous defender. It can also be run as a load option by having the tailback block the last man on the line of scrimmage and the quarterback optioned off the corner.

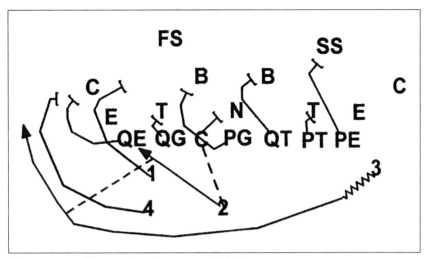

Diagram 8-3. Play 238 option versus 5-2-4

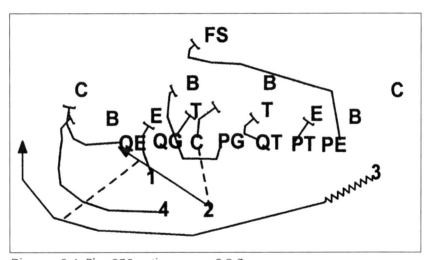

Diagram 8-4. Play 238 option versus 6-2-3

Coaching Points for Play 228

This play is run from a wing over formation and makes the defense adjust to the wing side. It is a very good power play and also sets up good action passes. The blocking back and quick end switch assignments on this play. The timing for the double-team with the wing works well with the quick end. Teams usually cheat their corner up against this formation, which gives the blocking back a better angle for this block. The tailback is the extra blocker and will block the first man that shows outside of the wing's block.

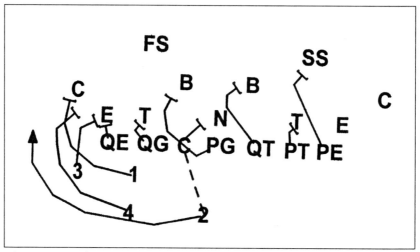

Diagram 8-5. Play 228 versus 5-2-4

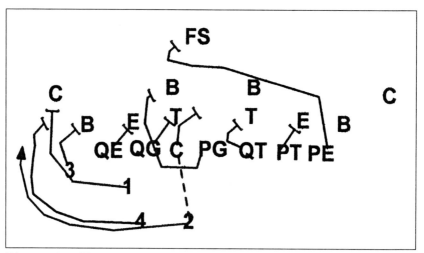

Diagram 8-6. Play 228 versus 6-2-3

Coaching Points for Play 232

This play comes off play 228 action and is similar to play 437, but going the opposite direction. Regular 2 hole blocking is used. Just as teams will adjust to the powerside, they will also adjust to the wing over formation, thus the reason for play 232. It is important that the line doesn't allow penetration, as the wing will be close to the line of scrimmage when he receives the ball. The quarterback must make the play look like play 228. The quarterback will give an inside handoff to the wing. The wing needs to take a jab or hesitation step, much as he does on play 235, for the timing to be correct.

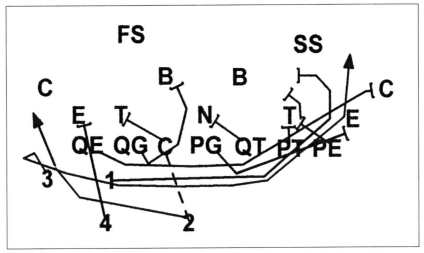

Diagram 8-7. Play 232 versus 5-2-4

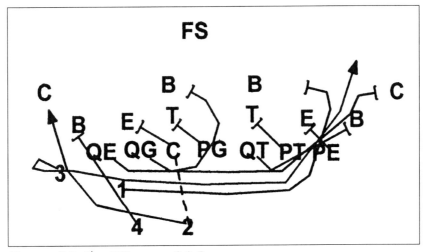

Diagram 8-8. Play 232 versus 6-2-3

Use of Formations

The use of formations is important and should be reiterated. Although not new plays, different formations can give the appearance of a new play. It is difficult enough for a team to prepare for the single wing, but using different formations and still run most of the base offense puts tremendous pressure on the defense. This advantage is tremendous for the offense. One example is play 241 read, which is one of base plays in the spin series. It can be run from the following formations: blue, blue flanker (power or quick), over, wing, wing over, pro, twins, twins over, and trey. And, wing motion can be added to any one of those formations to further compound the problems for the defense with just one play.

9

The Passing Game

Play-Action Passes

No matter what offense is run, unless vastly superior personnel are on the field, being able to throw the ball is necessary to keep the defense honest. The single wing offense is no different. As in the running game, the coach must be careful not to go crazy in drawing up pass plays. Obviously, the better the passer, the more passes the coach can install, with the only limits being his imagination. Following are examples of play-action passes in the single wing offense.

Coaching Points for Pass 241

This pass is a must to have in the offense. This play has the quarterback throw this pass by faking and then rolling out toward the receivers. However, the quarterback doesn't roll that way on any of the spin series runs, thus it can give a pass read key to the defense. Even though the quarterback throws most of the passes, the tailback throws this one. Many single wing teams have their tailback throw most of their passes, and most of the pass plays described here can be adjusted so that the tailback is the one doing the passing. The reason this pass is important in the offense is it will keep the defender responsible for flat coverage honest. Without it, that flat defender will be in the backfield as soon as he sees the tailback coming his way and will be very difficult to block. The tailback must make the play look like a run, and, in fact, the tailback is told, "If in doubt, run." The tailback will want to get a little more depth than he does on the run, but not so much that he tips the play to the defense. As he is carrying out his fake, he looks at the coverage: if the wing is open deep, he will throw to him right away; if the wing isn't open, he will throw to the blocking back in the flat. The blocking back should be no deeper than two yards off the line of scrimmage. He needs to get width, not depth, for two reasons. One, it forces the flat defender to cover him or he will be open immediately. If the flat defender does cover him, he will be out of the play. Second, if the blocking back is open, the tailback has an easy pass to throw because it is short. If the wing is covered deep and the blocking back is covered in the flat, a big hole exists in the defense between these receivers for the quick end's crossing route. The quick end should be at a depth of five to ten yards. This pass is also short and easy for the tailback to throw. The quick end will come into the tailback's view as the tailback is starting to turn up the field to run. If the quick end is open, he hits him with the pass. If the quick end is covered, the tailback just keeps on running as he would in play 241. The power end blocks on this play, so that the secondary gets a run read from him. The quarterback carries out his bootleg fake to keep the backside honest. Although a simple pass, this play is a must to have in the playbook.

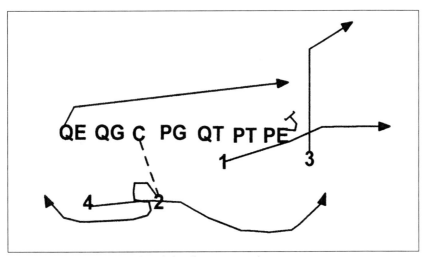

Diagram 9-1. Pass 241 (read the flat coverage)

Coaching Points for Pass 241 Throwback

This play looks exactly like pass 241. Two things are necessary for the play to be successful. One, the defense doesn't cover the quarterback on his bootleg fake. Second is a tailback that can throw the ball at least 25 to 30 yards. If these two factors are present, a big play is a strong possibility. If the quarterback is covered, the tailback will either run or throw the ball out of bounds.

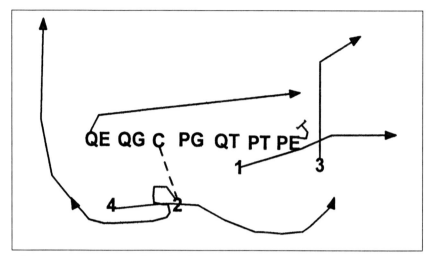

Diagram 9-2. Pass 241 throwback

Coaching Points for Pass 241 Boot

This pass is the foremost play-action in the single wing offense. The following coaching points make it work. The quarterback should not hurry his fake to the tailback. The quarterback should give the tailback a good hand fake and follow him with his head until the tailback has taken a few steps. This fake is necessary for the play to be successful. The fake allows the receivers to get open and also allows the blocking back to get position on the last man on the line of scrimmage for his block. The quick end should read the flat defender to his side, which is usually a corner. If the flat defender is blitzing, the quick end converts his flag route to an arrow route. On the arrow route, the quick end should turn, get his head to the quarterback immediately, and find the ball. The power end uses a slam release. On the slam release, the power end will give the defender over him a good pass block punch before he releases into his route. The power end's depth is five to ten yards deep. It is important that the wing gets depth on his post route and not run past the center's original alignment as he is breaking on the post route. If the wing doesn't get depth or runs too far across the field, one defender can cover both him and the power end or him and the quick end. After the quarterback makes his fake, he will roll behind the blocking back's block and find the flat defender. If this defender is blitzing, he will throw to the quick end immediately in the flat. If the defender isn't blitzing and not covering the quick end, he will throw to the quick end. If the quick end is covered, the quarterback will look for both the wing and the power end on their crossing routes and throw to the open receiver. If both are covered, the quarterback will run the ball. This play can also be called as a run play. When called as a run, everyone has the same responsibilities, except that the quarterback is going to run if the flat defender isn't on a blitz. This pass also can be run from many different formations, which causes the defense further problems.

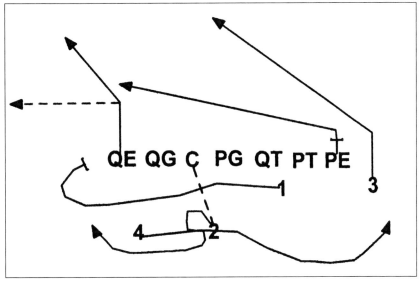

Diagram 9-3. Pass 241 boot

Coaching Points for Pass 241 Boot Throwback

This pass has the same game-breaking possibilities as 241 throwback pass. This pass is used more, primarily because the quarterback is a better passer in this scheme. As in 241 throwback, two things must be present for this pass to be successful. First, the tailback isn't being covered on his route as he fakes upfield. Second, the quarterback must be able to throw the ball about 30 yards.

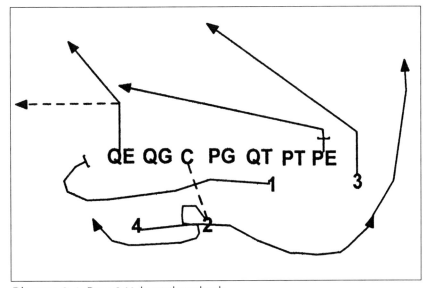

Diagram 9-4. Pass 241 boot throwback

Coaching Points for Pass 241 Read

After the 241 boot pass, this pass is the second most used in the in the play-action passing game. Although it can be run from the base set, it is usually run from the twins set. This play is also a formation that 241 read is run. The quarterback will make a good fake to the tailback, then step back, and throw. The quarterback's first read is the wing as he goes straight up the field. If the wing is covered, the quick end moves into this open area that the wing has cleared. This pass should be thrown quickly and has the potential to be a big play. It also keeps the backside honest, so that when play 241 read is run, the defenders from the backside aren't so quick to leave the receivers and pursue to the play.

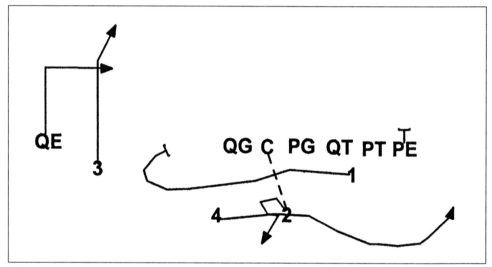

Diagram 9-5. Pass 241 read

Coaching Points for Pass 248

This pass is from the option play-action. The quarterback should take his first steps just as if he were running the option, then step back, and throw the ball. The routes for this pass are similar for the receivers to the routes run for pass 241 read. This pass can be run from many formations, but it is best when run from the twin set. The wing's route is the same as in pass 241 read. The quick end's route is different, in that he will run a quick hook route, instead of the in route. The reason for the hook is that the flow of the play is toward the quick end, and an in route would take him into the defensive pursuit. When teams are flying up to stop the option, this pass is very good to use.

Coaching Points for Pass 223

Of all the play-action passes, this play has the most big play potential. The quarterback should have a strong arm, but not necessarily an accurate one, because the ball will

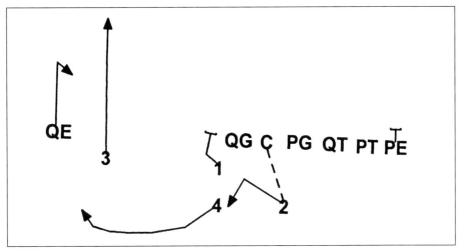

Diagram 9-6. Pass 248

be thrown 25 to 30 yards. The only receiver is the blocking back. He will sneak through the line and run to get behind the secondary. Since the blocking back usually isn't considered to be a receiver by the defense, the secondary may not see him coming out until it is too late. This play is best run in a non-passing situation. The wing and tailback should have great fakes to keep the secondary looking for the ball and allow the blocking back to slip behind the secondary. The quarterback can't hurry his fakes for the same reason. Since only one receiver is on this play, the quarterback will throw the ball away if the blocking back isn't open.

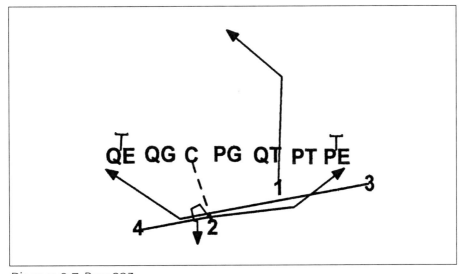

Diagram 9-7. Pass 223

Coaching Points for Pass 224

Of all the pass plays that come from the motion series, this play is the most consistent. This pass is especially effective against teams that don't rotate their secondary or make some other adjustment to the motion. The quick end runs deep to stretch the coverage vertically, and the quarterback will throw to him if open. If the quick end is covered, the quarterback will read the corner and throw to either the blocking back or the wing. This pass is difficult for the defense to cover, because of the three receivers.

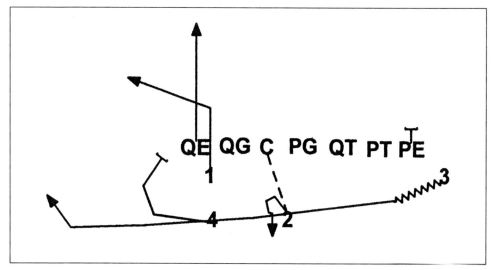

Diagram 9-8. Pass 224

Coaching Points for Pass 228

Although this pass is listed with the play-action passes, it is very close to being a sprint-out pass. The quarterback should make it look like the run before he shows pass. This play is a three-receiver pattern that is tough for the defense to cover. Depending on how the defense is covering the run will determine who is open on the pass. For example, if the corner is blitzing, the blocking back will be open. Or, if the corner covers the blocking back and the safety covers the wing, the quick end will be open. This pass is a play-action that can be run on passing downs without an outstanding passer. It is an easy pass for the quarterback to read, and if everyone is covered, he can run the ball and pick up positive yardage.

Coaching Points for Pass 441

This pass is the primary play-action from the power series. The key point is for the tailback to make it look like the run before he shows pass. This pass works well from

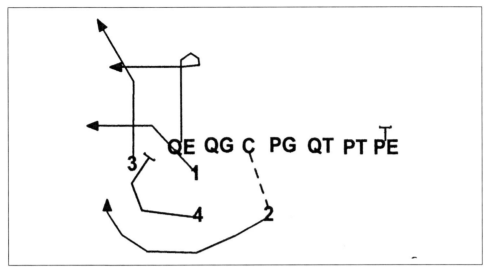

Diagram 9-9. Pass 228

the trey set, because it forces the defense to adjust to the strength of the formation, and then the ball is thrown opposite the strength of the set. Although the ball can be thrown to the quick end, it is usually thrown to the power end behind the linebackers that are running to stop play 441.The plays mentioned here are not the only play-action passes in the single wing offense; however, these passes are the most consistent because these passes can be completed by an average quarterback. These passes are necessary to have in the offense to take advantage of what the defense is trying to do to stop the running game.

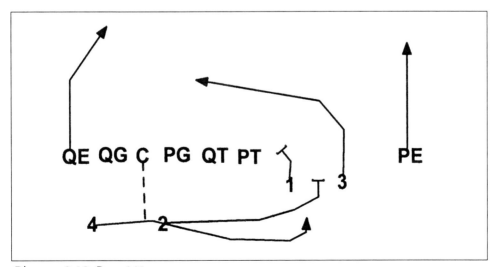

Diagram 9-10. Pass 441

Pass Situation Plays

In every game, situations will exist when the offense has to pass and the defense knows it has to pass. Although play-action passes can work in these situations, they aren't as effective as they are when thrown in non-passing situations. The following passes can be used with an average passer. Following are the six most consistent passes for these must-pass situations.

Coaching Points for Sprint Pass

This pass is easy for the quarterback to read, and, if the receivers are covered, the quarterback can run and pick up positive yardage. It is run from many formations, but usually run from an over set. This formation gives the defense a tight, run-looking set, but has two quick receivers to each side. The defense is forced to stay somewhat balanced, and usually only one defensive back exists to the quickside. The quarterback will sprint out to the quickside and read the defensive back. If the defensive back covers the quick end on his flag route, the quarterback looks for the blocking back in the flat. If both are covered, the quarterback will usually run, and, if the tailback is able to seal block the last man on the line of scrimmage, it becomes a foot race between the quarterback and a linebacker. The wing may be open on his route, if the defense covers the quick end and blocking back. All the wing has to do is get inside position on the powerside safety. If the coaches anticipate this type of coverage coming into the game, they should spend more practice time looking for the wing before running the ball. This pass is also good play to run from the pro set, as it really puts a lot of pressure on the safety to cover the blocking back in the flat or the quick end on his flag route.

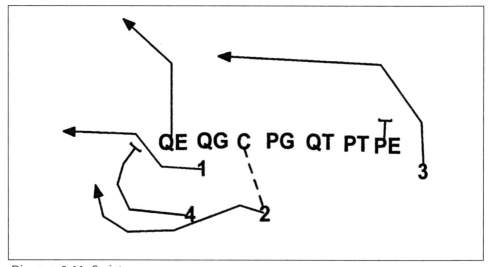

Diagram 9-11. Sprint pass

Coaching Points for Twins Pass

This pass is similar to the sprint pass. Different combination routes can be run with the quick end and wing, depending on the defense anticipated. This play also provides two blockers on the last man on the line of scrimmage, which enables the quarterback to almost always get outside the contain and put additional pressure on the defense. If the receivers are covered, the quarterback will put the ball away and run. Although many different combinations are possible with the receivers, the best is the quick end running a flag and the wing faking the post and running the out. The word "trail" tells the tailback to release for a pass after he blocks for a one to two count, after the quick end and wing clear out the area and the best running back gets the ball in space.

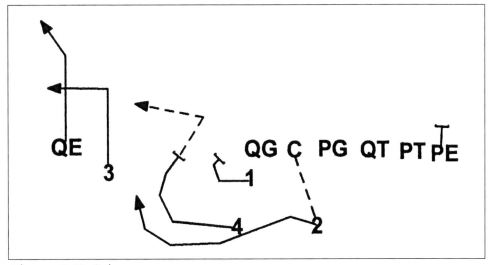

Diagram 9-12. Twins pass

Coaching Points for Trips Pass Curl and Dig

Many routes can be run from the trips set, however, the two basic routes are called curl and dig. The curl play puts pressure on the flat coverage. The wing runs a deep flag that the defender covering the deep outside one-third should cover. The quick end runs a curl deep enough to pick up the necessary yardage for the first down and makes eye contact with the quarterback. The quick end should slide in or out to get open after he runs his curl. The blocking back runs the arrow route. The quarterback will glance at the wing on his flag route and throw to him if he is open. The quarterback then reads the flat coverage and throws to the curl or the blocking back in the flat. If the quick end catches the ball, he should have enough yardage for the first down. If the receiver in the flat catches the ball, the quick end and wing turn back and block. The play looks almost like a punt return picket fence being set up if they get their blocks. The dig play puts pressure on the middle of the defense. The wing runs a deep post that the defender covering the deep middle one-third should cover. The quick end runs a deep in route, or dig, into the area cleared by the wing. The blocking back, or a substituted receiver, occupies the underneath coverage by running a short-curl route. If the underneath coverage drops deep enough to take away the dig route, the blocking back will be open. This play is an easy read for the quarterback, as all of the receivers are in his vision. The quarterback reads from the deep post, to the dig, to the curl. With an outstanding quarterback, the routes that can be run from the trips set are numerous, but the curl and the dig can be successful with an average passer.

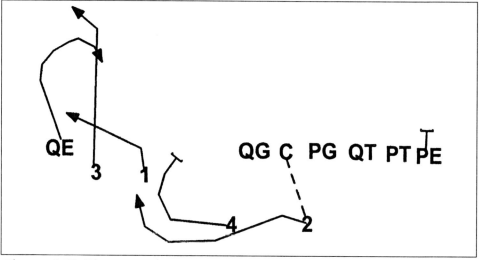

Diagram 9-13. Trips pass curl

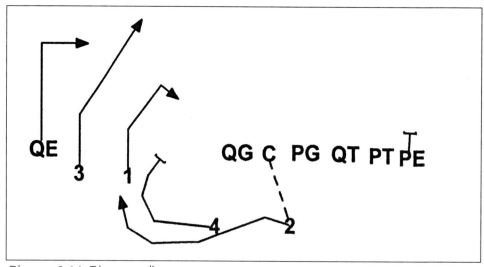

Diagram 9-14. Trips pass dig

Coaching Points for Ithaca Pass Slant, Curl, and Fade

This pass can be run from many different formations, but is usually run from the pro set versus a three-deep secondary and a twins set versus a two-deep secondary. The quarterback needs to get a lot of repetitions on this pass so that he can make the reads, but once he gets them down, this pass is almost unstoppable. The slant is the most frequently run route. The read of the quarterback is to throw the slant, or the curl, or fade, to the quick end. If the underneath coverage is taking away the slant, the quarterback looks to throw to the flaring tailback. The quarterback needs to realize who is taking away the slant, or curl, or fade, and then throw to the open receiver. Following is an example of reading the slant pass. If the outside linebacker is taking away the slant, the quarterback knows that he can hit the tailback on his flare route. This scenario is the most common. However, if the slant is being taken away by the inside linebacker, with the outside linebacker covering the tailback, the quarterback should find the power end as he crosses and replaces the inside linebacker. If the slant is being taken away by the safety, the tailback by the outside linebacker, and the power end by the inside linebacker, the quarterback should find the wing on his post route. Although the reads sound complicated, the quarterback can become very good at it with repetition. The pass is thrown very quickly and is an easy one for the line to block for.

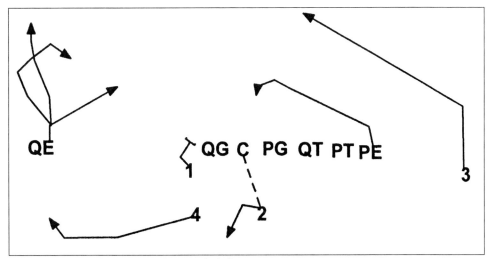

Diagram 9-15. Ithaca pass slant, curl, fade

Coaching Points for Deuce Pass

Deuce is a good pass to use in the hurry-up offense. The base route has the quick and power ends running fly routes up the hashes, with the tailback and wing running curls. Normally, however, a combination route is called to one side, with the opposite side end blocking and the wide out to that side running a deep post route. The blocking back will block to the side of the call. At least five minutes at each offensive practice should be spent on the hurry-up offense. During this time, the team should understand when to call timeouts, when the clock starts and stops, and when to execute the audible system. Sometimes, the coach may want to start a game in the hurry-up offense.

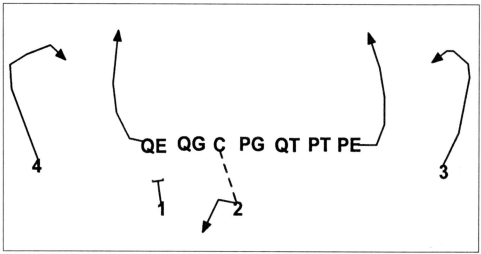

Diagram 9-16. Deuce pass

Screen Passes

Screens are an important part of any pass offense. Timing on the screen passes is very important, so practice time must be set aside to work on them. The time put in will be well worth it, because the screen pass can be the difference between victory and defeat. Following are five of the screen passes in the single wing offense.

Coaching Points for 241 Boot Screen

This play is the one screen that the offense should have in the game plan for every game. It comes off the best play-action pass and is thrown to the best running back. Everyone should make it look exactly like the 241 boot pass. The quarterback should look downfield before he throws to the tailback. It is extremely important that the quarterback looks to be sure that the tailback is open and doesn't throw before looking to prevent an interception. It is also very important that the tailback blocks his man before he releases for the pass. If the tailback doesn't block his man, the defender will ruin the timing on the play, and the play won't be successful. The line should block their man for a three count before releasing into the screen. The power guard will release upfield and block the most dangerous defender. The power tackle will release and block the most dangerous defender from the inside, setting up just outside the power end's original position. The quick tackle will release and block the corner. The rest of the line will execute their normal blocking assignments. It is important that they block like a normal pass.

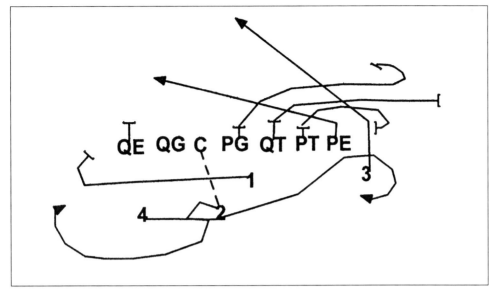

Diagram 9-17. 241 boot screen

Coaching Points for 224 Screen

The blocking on this screen is the same for the line as 241 boot screen. This screen comes off 224 motion action. This screen is very good against teams that rotate their secondary against the motion series. The pass goes to the blocking back. The blocking back should block before he releases for the pass, or his defender will mess up the timing of the play. As in the boot screen, the quarterback should be sure that the blocking back is open before he throws, to prevent an interception.

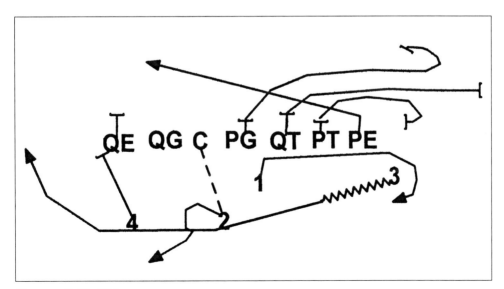

Diagram 9-18. 224 screen

Coaching Points for Trips Screen

The key point for this screen is patience by the quarterback. He should get depth as he brings the rush to him and before he throws the ball. By showing patience, the quarterback allows the receivers to clear out the area and the defensive linemen to take themselves out of the play. It is important that the receivers block the man covering them when the defender recognizes that the pass has been thrown. The line blocks for three counts before they release into the screen. The quick guard will release upfield and block the most dangerous defender. The center will block the most dangerous defender from the inside, as he sets up just outside the quick end's normal alignment. The power guard will release upfield and block the corner. The rest of the line will execute their normal pass blocking assignments. As stated earlier, they must block like a regular pass. The tailback will block his normal trips pass assignment and then release this defender so he can rush the quarterback and take himself out of the play.

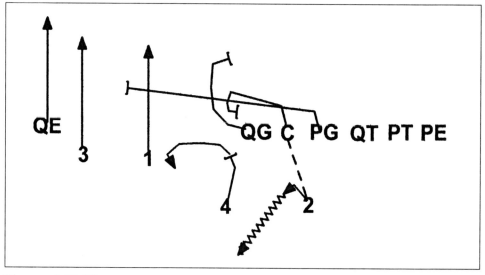

Diagram 9-19. Trips screen

Coaching Points for 223 Screen

Patience by the quarterback is key on this play. He should draw the defensive linemen to him before he passes the ball. He should get depth, but not make it obvious to the defensive linemen. The ends and backs going downfield should block the men covering them when the defenders recognize that the pass has been thrown. The quick guard, center, power guard, quick tackle, and power tackle should block for a three count before releasing their man. Then they form a tight wall and lead the blocking back upfield.

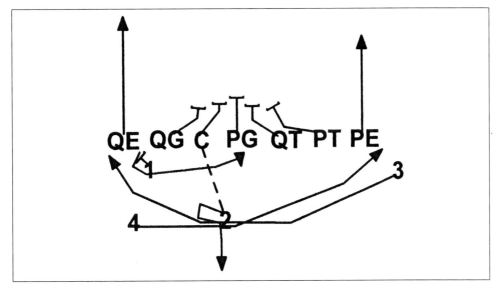

Diagram 9-20. 223 screen

Coaching Points for Bubble Screen

This play is run from a trips formation to the field. The quarterback throws the ball to the flaring tailback as quickly as he can. The tailback and blocking back switch positions on this play. The quick end and wing block the men covering them. The tailback bellies back a little to catch the ball and then runs for the sideline. The tailback should make every effort to get outside and not cut back. The quick end and wing should maintain their blocks in order for the play to be successful. If they get their blocks, the play becomes a foot race between the tailback and the rest of the defense.

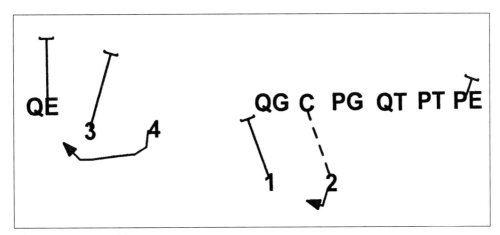

Diagram 9-21. Bubble screen

10

The Spread Single Wing

The spread offense with the quarterback in the shotgun position is nothing but a version of the single wing. It is simply the single wing from a spread formation. The single wing offense from a spread formation can take advantage of an outstanding passer without making a lot of changes to the offense. The run blocking rules can stay intact for the most part, with only minor adjustments. These changes allow the offense to run the ball from the spread set. The single wing already has some spread formations; therefore, very little new learning is necessary. Some minor pass blocking adjustments take place, but only slightly.

Spread Single Wing Formations

Diagrams 10-1 to 10-4 show the base formations in the spread single wing. Most are similar to the base single wing formations, except that the power end is split.

Running Plays from the Spread Single Wing

The main running plays in the spread sets are the power series, the motion series, 248 option, and 243 draw. For the most part, the blocking for the line is the same, with only minor adjustments, so it is very easy to run these plays from the spread sets.

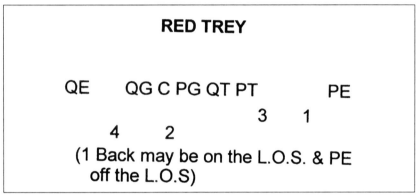

RED TRIPS

QE   QG C PG QT PT   PE

    1   3

      4   2

(1 Back may be on the L.O.S. & QE off the L.O.S.)

Diagram 10-1. Red trips—the back may be on the line of scrimmage, and the quick end off the line of scrimmage.

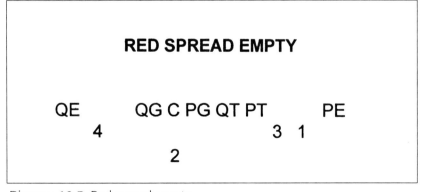

RED TREY

QE   QG C PG QT PT   PE

          3   1

    4   2

(1 Back may be on the L.O.S. & PE off the L.O.S)

Diagram 10-2. Red trey—the back may be on the line of scrimmage and the power end off the line of scrimmage.

RED SPREAD EMPTY

QE   QG C PG QT PT   PE

  4   3   1

      2

Diagram 10-3. Red spread empty

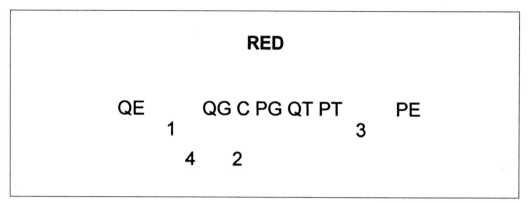

Diagram 10-4. Red

Coaching Points for Play 442

Play 442 is one of the best running plays from the spread formations. Although it can be run from the base red spread formation, it should be run more from the red spread trips formation, because it removes a defender from the point of attack. The only line blocking adjustment is with the quick guard. Instead of turning past the center to block the backside linebacker, he blocks the first lineman past the center to his outside. The key block on the play is from the 2 back. He should get the playside linebacker. This block is easy if the linebacker blitzes, but a tougher block if the linebacker flows with the play and fills at the hole. The 4 back should make the play look like 441 and then cut up behind the trap block of the pulling lineman the same way he does in the base 442 play. This play is tough for the defense to stop, because little or no secondary help exists.

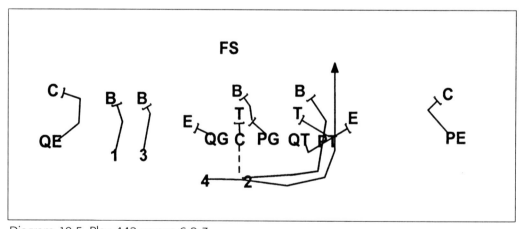

Diagram 10-5. Play 442 versus 6-2-3

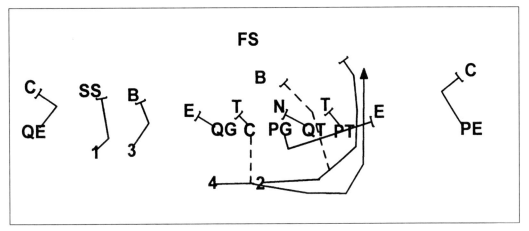

Diagram 10-6. Play 442 versus 5-3-3

Coaching Points for Play 435

Although diagramed from the red spread, this play should be run more from the red spread trey set, because it removes a defender from the point of attack. As shown by the dotted lines, the 1 back can go in motion to block the last man on the line of scrimmage so that he will not interfere with the handoff. No line blocking adjustments are needed for the play, so no new learning exists for the linemen. The only adjustment made is with the 3 back's alignment. The timing of the play is critical; therefore, the 3 back should align so that he can be at the right spot for the handoff from the 4 back. Because this play comes off 442 action, which is a fast-flow play, the linebackers usually take themselves out of the play.

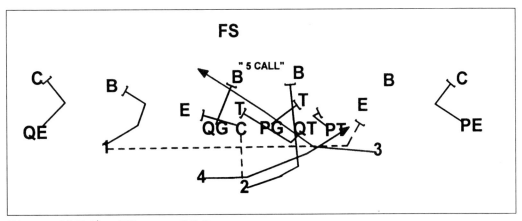

Diagram 10-7. Play 435 versus 6-2-3

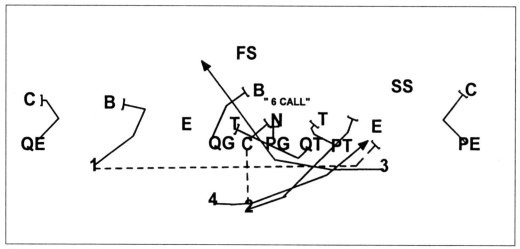

Diagram 10-8. Play 435 versus 5-2-4

Coaching Points for Play 238 Motion

Since motion is used a lot in the spread single wing to create new formations, this play is a natural to run. No new learning needs to take place. In fact, the spread set provides better angles for some of the blocks, thus making it an easier play to execute. The 2 back should time his cadence so that the 3 back doesn't have to slow down as he sprints past the 2 back.

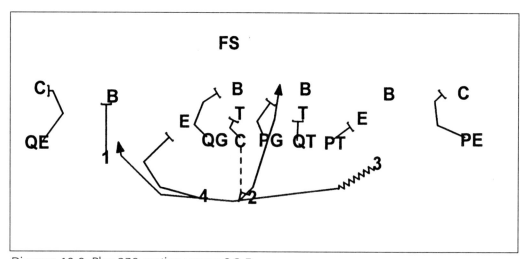

Diagram 10-9. Play 238 motion versus 6-2-3

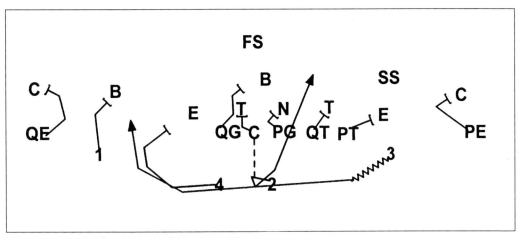

Diagram 10-10. Play 238 motion versus 5-3-3

Coaching Points for Play 223 Motion

This play is good play, especially when teams chase the motion man. The line blocking for this play changes, because on base 3 hole plays the 1 back does the trapping. The power tackle's block is the first man to his outside. The quick tackle's block is the first lineman past the power guard. The power guard's block is the first lineman past the center. The center's block is the first lineman head-up to backside. The quick guard's block is to pull and lead through the hole, blocking the playside linebacker. As in the base 223 motion play, the fake between the 2 back and the 3 back is crucial for the success of the play. The quick guard should get the playside linebacker, whether he blitzes or not. Due to the motion and fake, this block is not as difficult as it may appear. As in other spread single wing plays, if the block on the linebacker is made, little secondary support exists.

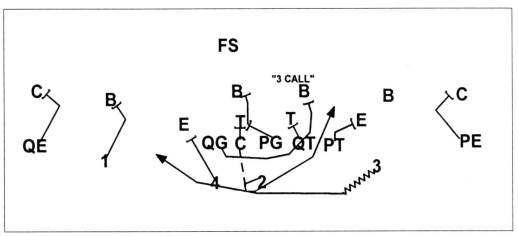

Diagram 10-11. Play 223 motion versus 6-2-3

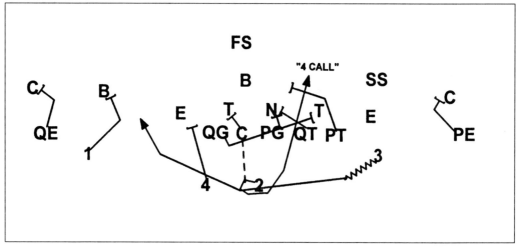

Diagram 10-12. Play 223 motion versus 5-3-3

Coaching Points for Play 248

This play is good from the base sets, but it is even better from the spread sets. Although diagrammed from the base red spread set, this play should be run more from a red spread trey set to eliminate a defender. When run from the red spread set, the quick guard blocks the linebacker. This play is especially successful against teams that use man-to-man coverage, because it makes containing very difficult. As in 238 motion, the line has no new responsibilities to learn.

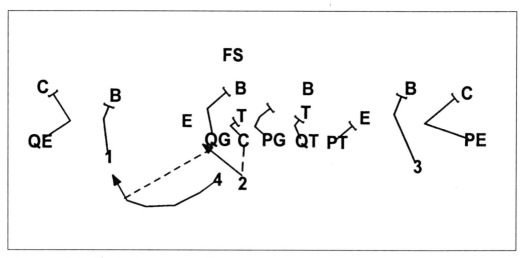

Diagram 10-13. Play 248 versus 6-2-3

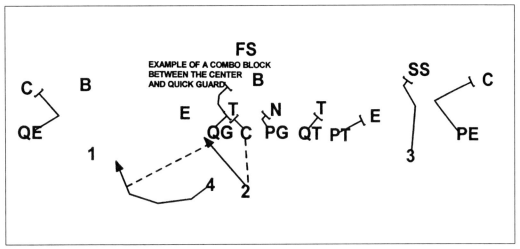

Diagram 10-14. Play 248 versus 5-3-3

Coaching Points for Play 243 Draw

As in spread 223 motion, the line should use their spread 3 hole blocking rules. The 3 back will motion across and block the last man on the line of scrimmage to protect the handoff. The technique of the play is the same as in the base single wing. 243 draw is a good surprise play when the defense is looking for a pass.

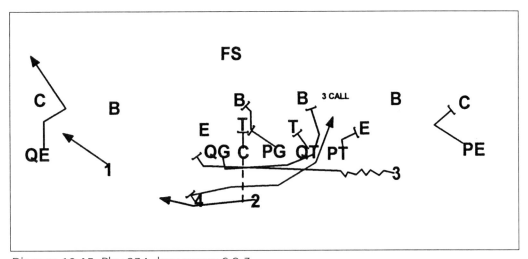

Diagram 10-15. Play 234 draw versus 6-2-3

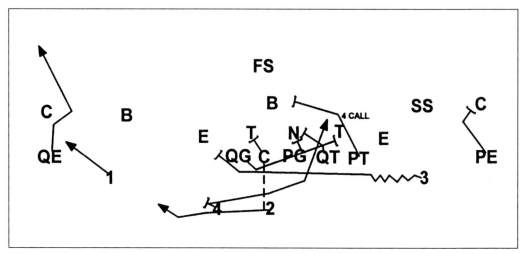

Diagram 10-16. Play 234 draw versus 5-3-3

Passing from the Spread Single Wing

Stopping both the runs and pass from the spread formations is very difficult for the defense, particularly versus a good throwing quarterback. In fact, with a good quarterback and the threat of the pass, the running game becomes even better because of lack of secondary support. To make the spread single wing effective, the threat of the pass must be present, so that the defense is forced to play honest.

Slight adjustments in the pass blocking rules are necessary when in the spread single wing. Following are the changes for each of the positions. The quick guard will block the first lineman from his outside shoulder to the inside. (In the base, he had the second). The center will block the second lineman from outside the quick guard to the inside. (In the base, he had the third). The power guard will block the third lineman from outside the power tackle to the inside. If no third lineman exists, block the first linebacker from the power tackle to the inside if he blitzes. If he doesn't blitz, help out with the most dangerous defender. (In the base, he had the fourth man from the quick end's side). The quick tackle will block the second lineman from outside the power tackle to the inside. (In the base, he had the first man past the power guard). The power tackle will block the first lineman from his outside to the inside. (In the base, he had the second man past the power guard). The 4 back will block the first linebacker from the quick guard to the inside. If he doesn't blitz, help out with the most dangerous defender. (In the base, the 4 back didn't have a set pass blocking rule). Switches are possible between linemen if it gives them a better angle. The power guard also has a "rock" call if 4 linemen exist from outside the power tackle to his inside gap. This call is rare but could happen against a six-man line. On a "rock" call, the power guard, quick tackle, and the power tackle each block the first lineman to their inside. Changes occur in the blocking, because the 1 back, power end, and quick end are not involved in the blocking. A big reason for these changes is the fact that only a few defensive alignments can be used to cover each of the receivers. Most of the time, the defense will only have a six-man front. Although a seven-man front is seldom used, it is possible that the defense will gamble and run a seven-man front against the spread single wing. The reason a seven-man front is not often used is that to cover every receiver, no safety is free. As mentioned in the running game, 248 option or 238 motion are very effective running plays against man-to-man coverage because no contain. Also quick crossing passes such as 2-3, which will be explained, are also very effective versus man-to-man coverage. However, to pass versus a seven-man front, one free or unblocked defender will exist. The quarterback should know this and get rid of the ball quickly. Diagrams 10-17 and 10-18 illustrate the main six- and seven-man defensive fronts seen by the spread offense and examples of pass blocking for each front.

As can be seen in the diagrams, a bootleg pass can also be thrown from spread sets. As in the base single wing set, many play-action passes can be run from the spread single wing set. The only limitation is the coach's imagination and the limitation of practice time. Also, the use of screen passes, and an automatic screen, fit better with the spread single wing than play-action passes. Following are diagrams of the spread single wing screen passes.

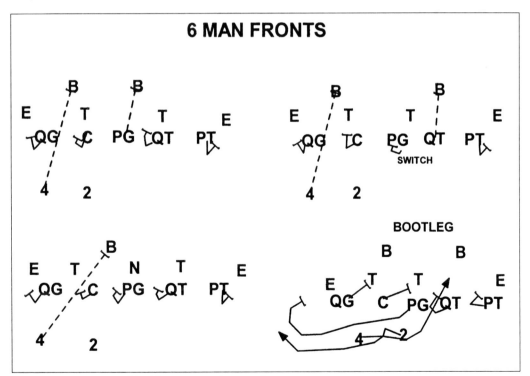

Diagram 10-17. Pass blocking versus six-man fronts

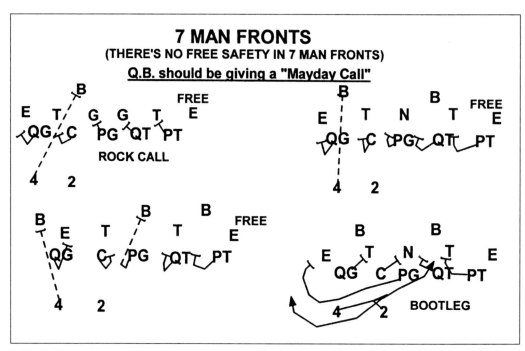

Diagram 10-18. Pass blocking versus seven-man fronts

Coaching Points for the Screen Passes

The 241 boot screen comes off the best play-action pass. Two keys are necessary to make the play work. The first is that the 2 back should not hurry his fake to the 4 back. He must sit and wait as the 4 back goes by him, give him a good hand ride, and turn his head to watch the 4 back run, before he bootlegs out to throw the screen. This timing allows the blocking to be set up, especially the power guard's. The second key is that the 4 back must block the first man outside of the power tackle, to allow the 2 back to make an excellent fake, and still have time to set up for the screen pass.

The trips screen is very easy to install because the line uses their spread 3 hole blocking rules. One key to the play is that the 2 back should be a good actor and draw the defensive linemen to him. Another key is that the 4 back should aggressively block the first lineman outside the quick guard, so that he thinks it is a pass and doesn't get in the way of the 3 back coming behind the line for the pass.

The spread screen is also a timing play. As in the trips screen, the 2 back should draw the defensive linemen deep so they cannot catch the play from behind. The 4 back blocks the same man as he does on the trips screen, but uses a screen-block technique that allows the defender to get by him. The quick guard's block on the

SCREEN PASSES

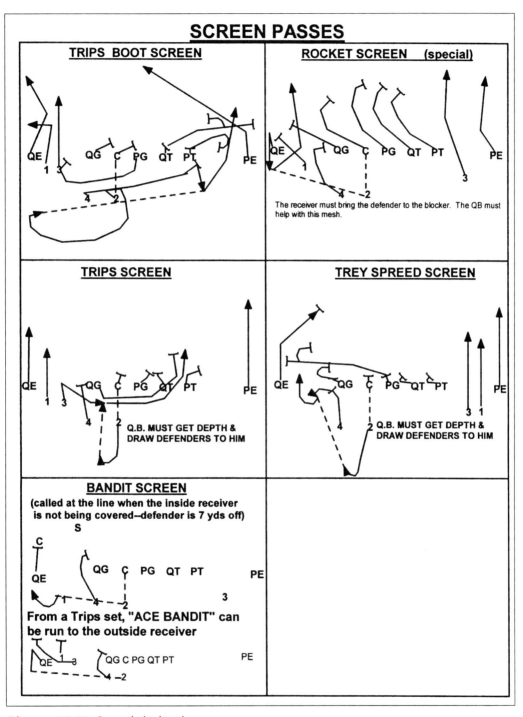

TRIPS BOOT SCREEN

QE   QG   C   PG   QT   PT   PE

ROCKET SCREEN   (special)

QE   QG   C   PG   QT   PT   PE

The receiver must bring the defender to the blocker. The QB must help with this mesh.

TRIPS SCREEN

QE   QG   C   PG   QT   PT   PE

Q.B. MUST GET DEPTH &
DRAW DEFENDERS TO HIM

TREY SPREED SCREEN

QE   QG   C   PG   QT   PT   PE

Q.B. MUST GET DEPTH &
DRAW DEFENDERS TO HIM

BANDIT SCREEN

(called at the line when the inside receiver
is not being covered--defender is 7 yds off)

S

C

QE   QG   C   PG   QT   PT   PE

From a Trips set, "ACE BANDIT" can
be run to the outside receiver

QE   QG C PG QT PT   PE

Diagram 10-19. Spread single wing screen passes

linebacker and power guard's seal to the inside are important, but the downfield blocks of the quick end and 1 back will determine whether it will be a big play or not.

The key to the rocket screen is getting the ball to the quick end (or power end) as quickly as possible. The 2 back doesn't need to have the strings to throw the pass. No style points exist on this play. All he has to do is catch the snap, and as quickly as possible get the ball to the wide receiver. The entire offensive line will release downfield immediately on the snap. None of them block anyone on the line of scrimmage, but block downfield. Another reason is that the 2 back must get rid of the ball in a hurry. If executed properly, it almost looks like a punt return wall for the receiver.

The last screen is not a called play in the huddle. Anytime an uncovered inside receiver exists, the 2 back has the option of throwing him the ball. The 2 back will give the receiver a signal and, like the rocket screen, get the ball to the receiver as quickly as possible. It is important that the receiver run to the outside and away from the defenders. The outside receiver should see the signal and block the man on him.

These screens are an important part of the spread single wing. Due to the fact that the spread single wing looks like passing formations, the screens are easy to set up and can result in many big plays for the offense.

The Passing Tree

A passing tree (Diagram 10-20) is used in the spread single wing. Almost all of the pass plays use the passing tree to tell the receivers what route to run. To change the routes in the passing tree, simply place a 1 in front of the number. For example, instead of 6 make it 16, and the route is run deeper. Following are the possible changes:

> 11 = 10-yard hitch
> 12 = 4- to 6-yard slant
> 13 = Run the arrow and turn the route into a wheel route
> 14 = 15-yard in route (dig route)
> 15 = 15-yard out route
> 16 = Curl route run 15 yards back to 13 yards
> 17 = 15-yard flag route
> 18 = 15-yard post route (seam route)
> 19 = Fade route

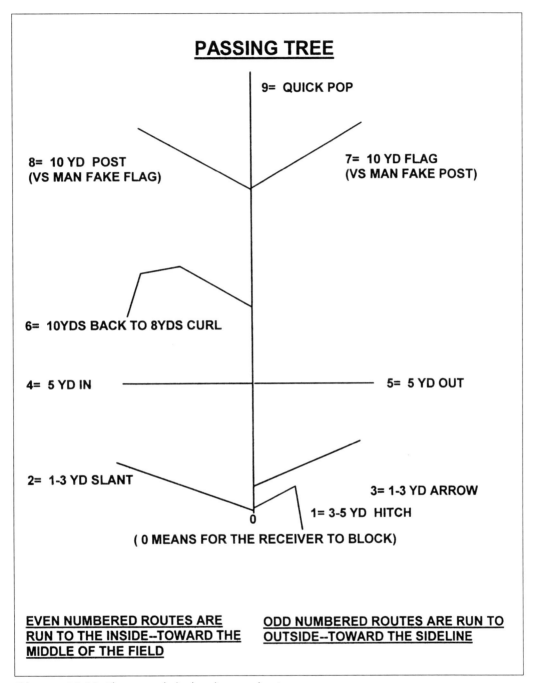

Diagram 10-20. The spread single wing passing tree

Another way to change the routes is to give a number after the route number, done only with the 2 and 3 routes. For example, instead of 2 make it 25, and the receiver would run the 2 route, then break it off, and turn it into a 5 route.

Word tags are another way to change routes in the passing tree. The first word tag is "stop." For example, if facing a squat corner in a cover two defensive look, a 3 route would run the receiver right into the defender. In this case, call a 3 stop route. The receiver would run his 3 route and then stop or sit down in the open space in the defense. The other word tag used is "go." For example, if facing a defender that is jumping the 1 route, the route is changed to a 1 go. This call would turn the hitch route into a hitch-and-go route. A word tag that doesn't change the routes, but changes the alignment, is "ace." When ace is called, the ends move off the line of scrimmage, and the 1 back and 3 back move onto the line of scrimmage. This technique allows the ends to be put in motion. Ace can also give better angles to run some of the crossing routes. The other word tags apply to the 4 back. Any tag at the end of a route is applied to the 4 back. One example is, "Quick-7-5-flare." With this tag, the 4 back would run his flare route instead of blocking. Diagram 10-21 illustrates the 4 back's word tag routes.

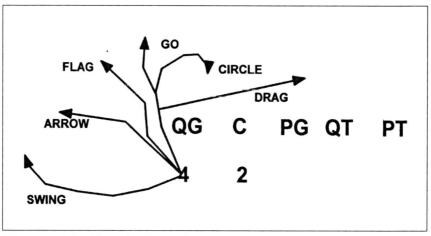

Diagram 10-21. The 4 backs word tag routes

The 2 back calls the pass play in the following sequence. First, the 2 back will give the side, either quick or power. Next, he will give the routes. The routes always start with the outside receiver to the inside receiver. For example, in, "Pass quick-7-5," the quick end would run a 7 route (flag), and the 1 back would run a 5 route (out). If in a trips formation, the call could be, "Pass 6-3-7," which would have the quick end run a 6 (curl), the 1 back run a 3 (arrow), and the 3 back run a 7 (flag). If the 2 back wanted to throw to the one receiver side in a trips or trey formation, he would only give one number, and the single receiver side becomes the primary route. One example is, "Pass trey-19." Mirrored routes are not used because it is too difficult for a

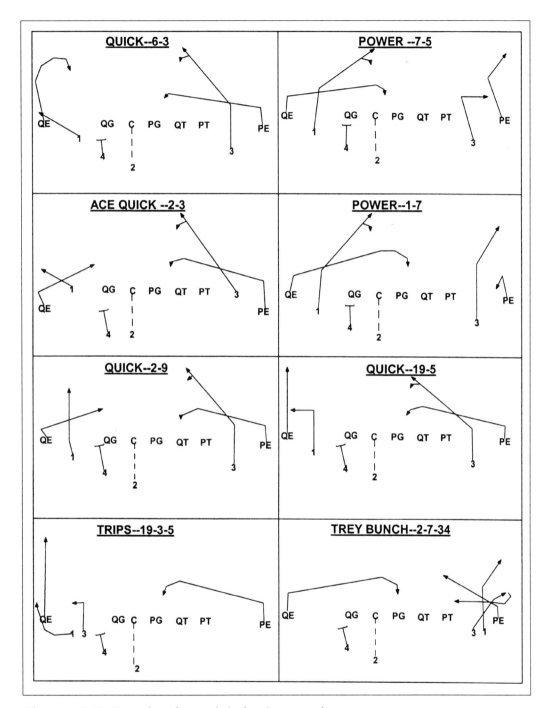

Diagram 10-22. Examples of spread single wing pass plays

quarterback to read one side of the defense and, if the receiver is covered, try to turn and read the opposite side. Not only are mirrored routes difficult for the quarterback, but it takes a lot of time, which makes it tough for the line to hold their blocks long enough for the quarterback to read both sides. The 2 back should throw the ball in 2.5 seconds or less. If he takes any longer, he could be sacked. During practice, a good idea is to have a coach with a stopwatch time the 2 back. Instead of mirrored routes, pre-set backside routes exist. The receivers on the backside will run an 18-16 route and a box route. They can determine which one will run which route. The 18-16 route is a route run at the middle safety. If no middle safety exists, the receiver will run the 18 route (deep post). If a safety is in the middle, the receiver will run the 16 route (deep curl) in front of him. The box route is a blitz control route. The receiver will run to an area between the quick guard and power tackle, sit down in the open space, and make himself available to the 2 back. Thus, the 2 back knows he has two backside receivers if the primary routes are covered. He can see both of them very quickly. If they are covered, he should run or throw the ball away. Diagram 10-22 illustrates some examples of called routes.

Hopefully, what this chapter has shown is the versatility of the single wing. If coaches don't want to tell people they are running the single wing, the coach can do like many college coaches do today and make up a name for the offense. Just remember: "A rose is a rose."

11

The Secret Weapon

The single wing's secret weapon can average close to 50 yards an attempt. It can be the difference between many wins and losses. What is this play? It is the quick kick. Don't underestimate the power of this play, especially in close games, because the quick kick can change field position and lead to that all-important score. Not many plays are going to average close to 50 yards an attempt.

Following are some guidelines on when to use this play. During the season, every team has some situations where it is third down and forever. Very few plays are designed to pick up the amount of yardage that is needed. Usually, the best that can be expected is to gain some yardage and punt on fourth down. This situation is one to use the quick kick. Most teams never have a punter that can consistently punt the ball 50 yards, but this yardage is the normal result of the quick kick. Another situation that is good for the quick kick is the complete opposite, when in a fourth-and-short situation. The defense isn't sure if the offense is going to go for it or not. The formation shows the defense that the offense is going to go for it, so the defense has to prepare to stop the short-yardage play. The 50 yard kick puts the defense in the hole. Another situation for the quick kick is on nights when the game is being played in terrible weather, especially heavy winds. The quick kick may not go 50 yards in terrible weather, but will probably average more than a normal punt.

One technique used for the quick kick is the rocker method to get the kick off. The ball is snapped to the quarterback, he takes about a quarter turn, rocks back, and kicks the ball. Another technique is to have the quarterback take three steps back, just prior to the snap, receive the snap, and kick the ball. This technique accomplishes a couple of things. Most importantly, it makes the kick safer because the kicker is further from the line of scrimmage when he kicks the ball. Also, the kicker is allowed to kick the ball at a lower angle, which gives more roll on the kick after it hits the ground. The threat of the quick kick also sets up the fake quick kick plays. As soon as the defense sees the quarterback dropping back, they need to react. For example, safeties can run to get depth, linemen will either rush with reckless abandon or just stand up and watch. The defense can make other adjustments. These reactions allow the offense to run fake quick kick plays. One of the best fake quick kick plays is play 444 power. This play is usually successful because defensive linemen have a tendency to play softer when they think the play is a quick kick. This fact makes it easy for the offensive linemen to knock them off the line of scrimmage for a positive play. When the defensive line is really charging, a 5 hole or 6 hole play to trap the aggressive charging linemen is usually a good play. Pass plays can also be run from quick kick action. One of the best passes is a pop pass to either the quick end or wing to take advantage of the safeties running out of their coverage area. The quick end and wing release on the quick kick, so it doesn't give the pass away. These runs or passes are done on third-down situations for the most part, so even if they aren't successful, the offense can still punt on fourth down.

The blocking used for the quick kick is the same for the line as their pass blocking assignments, with the power end blocking also. The tailback will block the first man from the outside shoulder of the quick end to the inside. The blocking back will block the most dangerous defender to the side of the kicker's kicking foot. The quick end and wing release and cover the kick.

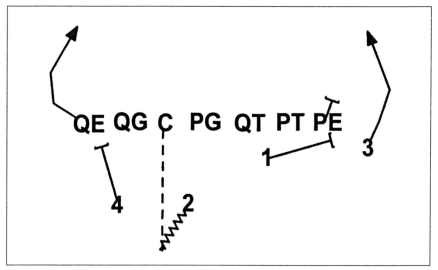

Diagram 11-1. The quick kick

Conclusion

The single wing is a great system of football. However, one thing is important: football teams are made up of people, and people make the system go. The coach must work with his players to be sure they are fundamentally sound. Blocking and tackling still win games, no matter what the system. The single wing will give a team a chance to win, even without the superstars; but the coach's duty is to prepare them for the game so they can do what is asked of them.

This text only scratches the surface of the single wing. As stated at the beginning of the book, many others are more qualified to write this book. However, any coach that wanted to run the offense has a place to start. If nothing else, maybe this book has provided a stimulus for thought. The information in this book is what is done at Ithaca High School. If readers have questions about anything after reading this book, feel free to write or call Ithaca High School, in Ithaca, Michigan. Good luck to coaches and teams in the future, and, hopefully, the single wing is good for the teams that use it.

About the Author

Jim Ahern is the offensive coordinator at Palmetto Ridge High School in Naples, Florida. Previously, he was the head football coach at Ithaca High School in Ithaca, Michigan, for 34 years. He began his coaching career at Hackett High School, in Kalamazoo, Michigan, under hall of fame head coach Dick Soisson. Ahern's next stop was at North Branch High School, in North Branch, Michigan, where he worked under another hall of fame coach, Don Smeznic. Ahern became the head coach at Gobles High School, in Gobles, Michigan, in 1969. After three years at Gobles, Ahern moved to his position at Ithaca.

Prior to his move to Florida in 2004, Ahern was very active in the Michigan High School Football Coaches Association. As the Playoff Committee Chairman of the MHSFCA, he was very proactive in getting the state of Michigan to begin state football playoffs and expanding the playoffs to their present level. He was the president of the MHSFCA in 1990. Ahern had the privilege to coach in the state of Michigan's high school all-star game in 1991. Ahern has been the recipient of many coaching awards, with the highlights being in 1996 when Ahern was inducted into the Michigan High School Football Coaches Association Hall of Fame and in 2002 when he was chosen as the Michigan High School Coaches Association Football Coach of the Year.